Harrogate Colle

Case Studies   ganisational Change

ALT Re-Source
Collection

LEEDS METROPOLITAN UNIVERSITY

LIBRARY ONLY

Leeds Metropolitan University

17 0472852 0

LEEDS METROPOLITAN
UNIVERSITY
LIBRARY
1704728570
UNI-ALT
GEN-7951
IS-P06
658·314 LEW

Work–Life Integration
Case Studies of Organisational Change

Suzan Lewis
Manchester Metropolitan University, UK

and

Cary L. Cooper
University of Lancaster, UK

John Wiley & Sons, Ltd

Copyright © 2005   John Wiley & Sons Ltd, The Atrium, Southern Gate, Chichester,
West Sussex PO19 8SQ, England

Telephone (+44) 1243 779777

Email (for orders and customer service enquiries): cs-books@wiley.co.uk
Visit our Home Page on www.wiley.com

All Rights Reserved. No part of this publication may be reproduced, stored in a retrieval system or
transmitted in any form or by any means, electronic, mechanical, photocopying, recording, scanning or
otherwise, except under the terms of the Copyright, Designs and Patents Act 1988 or under the terms of
a licence issued by the Copyright Licensing Agency Ltd, 90 Tottenham Court Road, London W1T 4LP, UK,
without the permission in writing of the Publisher. Requests to the Publisher should be addressed
to the Permissions Department, John Wiley & Sons Ltd, The Atrium, Southern Gate, Chichester, West
Sussex PO19 8SQ, England, or emailed to *permreq@wiley.co.uk*, or faxed to (+44) 1243 770620.

Designations used by companies to distinguish their products are often claimed as trademarks. All brand
names and product names used in this book are trade names, service marks, trademarks or registered
trademarks of their respective owners. The Publisher is not associated with any product or vendor mentioned
in this book.

This publication is designed to provide accurate and authoritative information in regard to the subject
matter covered. It is sold on the understanding that the Publisher is not engaged in rendering
professional services. If professional advice or other expert assistance is required, the services of a
competent professional should be sought.

Other Wiley Editorial Offices

John Wiley & Sons Inc., 111 River Street, Hoboken, NJ 07030, USA

Jossey-Bass, 989 Market Street, San Francisco, CA 94103-1741, USA

Wiley-VCH Verlag GmbH, Boschstr. 12, D-69469 Weinheim, Germany

John Wiley & Sons Australia Ltd, 33 Park Road, Milton, Queensland 4064, Australia

John Wiley & Sons (Asia) Pte Ltd, 2 Clementi Loop #02-01, Jin Xing Distripark, Singapore 129809

John Wiley & Sons Canada Ltd, 22 Worcester Road, Etobicoke, Ontario, Canada M9W 1L1

Wiley also publishes its books in a variety of electronic formats. Some content that appears in print
may not be available in electronic books.

Library of Congress Cataloging-in-Publication Data

Lewis, Suzan.
  Work-life integration : case studies of organizational change / Suzan Lewis and Cary L. Cooper
    p. cm.
  ISBN 0-470-85344-1 (hbk) – ISBN 0-470-85343-3 (pbk)
  1. Work and family – Case studies.   2. Organizational change – Case studies.
  I. Cooper, Cary L.   II. Title.
  HD904.25.L48 2005
  306.3'6 – dc22   2004022951

British Library Cataloguing in Publication Data

A catalogue record for this book is available from the British Library

ISBN 0-470-85344-1 (hbk)
ISBN 0-470-85343-3 (pbk)

Project management by Originator, Gt Yarmouth, Norfolk (typeset in 11/13pt Times)
Printed and bound in Great Britain by TJ International Ltd, Padstow, Cornwall
This book is printed on acid-free paper responsibly manufactured from sustainable forestry
in which at least two trees are planted for each one used for paper production.

Contents

About the Authors

PROFESSOR SUZAN LEWIS

Suzan Lewis is Professor of Organizational and Work–Life Psychology at Manchester Metropolitan University, and a Director of the Work–Life Research Centre. She is a founding editor of the international journal *Community, Work and Family*. Since the 1980s she has been researching and writing about work and personal life issues, with a particular focus on workplace flexibility and culture and organisational change. She has directed many national and international research projects on work–personal life issues including a current EU study of "gender, parenthood and the changing European workplace". The numerous publications of which she is author or co-author include, for example, *Dual-Earner Families: International Perspectives* (Sage, 1992), *The Work–Family Challenge: Rethinking Employment* (Sage, 1996) and *Young Europeans, Work and Family* (Sage, 2002). She has also undertaken consultancy and training on work–personal life issues, flexible working and organisational change in the UK, USA and Japan.

PROFESSOR CARY L. COOPER, CBE

Cary L. Cooper is Professor of Organizational Psychology and Health, Lancaster University Management School and Pro-Vice-Chancellor (External Relations) at Lancaster University. He is the author of over 100 books (on occupational stress, women at work, and industrial and organisational psychology), has written over 400 scholarly articles for academic journals, and is a frequent contributor to national newspapers, TV and radio. He is currently founding editor of the *Journal of Organizational Behavior* and co-editor of the medical journal *Stress and Health* (formerly *Stress Medicine*). He is a Fellow of the British Psychological Society, the Royal Society of Arts, the Royal Society of Medicine, the Royal Society of Health and an Academician of the Academy for the Social Sciences. Professor Cooper is the President of the British Academy of Management, is a Companion of the Chartered Management Institute and one of the first UK-based Fellows of the (American) Academy of Management (having also won the 1998 Distinguished Service Award for his contribution to management science from the Academy of Management). In 2001, he was awarded a CBE in the Queen's Birthday Honours List for his contribution to organisational health. He holds Honorary Doctorates from Aston University (DSc), Heriot-Watt University (DLitt), Middlesex University (Doc. Univ) and Wolverhampton University (DBA).

Professor Cooper is the editor (jointly with Professor Chris Argyris of Harvard Business School) of the international scholarly *Blackwell Encyclopedia of Management* (12-volume set), and the editor of *Who's Who in the Management Sciences*. He has been an advisor to two UN agencies: the World Health Organization and the International Labour Organisation; he published a major report for the EU's European Foundation for the Improvement of Living and Work Conditions on *Stress Prevention in the Workplace*; and is a special advisor to the Defence Committee of the House of Commons on their Duty of Care enquiry. Professor Cooper is also the President of the Institute of Welfare Officers, Vice-President of the British Association for Counselling and Psychotherapy, an Ambassador of the Samaritans and Patron of the National Phobic Society.

Foreword

by Professor Ronald J. Burke

Interest in the interplay of work and family has increased steadily over the past 20 years. What was historically seen as a woman's issue has come to occupy an important concern for men, families and organisations. Men have families too and organisations employ men and women with lives outside of the workplace.

Several broad and widespread demographic and economic factors have increased the salience of work and family. There are now more women in the workforce. There are more dual-earner families as well as more single-parent households. There has simultaneously been an intensification of work. More women and men are working longer hours and reporting greater demands in their workplaces. The downsized, restructured, outsourced, networked and allianced organisation now requires more from fewer employees as they struggle with heightened worldwide competition, and more demanding customers in an environment where speed and cost have become more important. Technological and telecommunications advancements have made it possible to work 24/7 from anywhere. Work and family have become particularly problematic for managers and professionals performing knowledge work—an increasing percentage of the workforce. These employees now work harder to maintain family income in response to uncertain feelings about their future security and to keep up with or ahead of the Joneses. Work and family has become a pressing concern for men, women, families and organisations as a result.

Our views on work and family have also evolved and developed during this time. The early writers viewed the two spheres as conflicting—work conflicts with family and family conflicts with work. Not surprisingly, the research showed work–family conflict to be more widespread and have a more negative impact on employees than did family–work conflict.

The first proposed solution to the problem of conflict was the notion of work–family balance: work and family should be balanced. Balance, as a concept, became problematic for some, however, since balance suggests a 50/50 investment. Some individuals might find balance in a 60/40 arrangement.

In addition, achieving balance implies taking away from one sphere and applying it to the other. Balance also suggested a similar solution for everyone—a 50/50 investment. Balance also suggests that work is not a part of one's life but something separate. The balance notion also leads to a quick-fix solution to work–family conflict.

More current thinking frames the work–family issue in terms of integration or harmonisation. These terms legitimise a number of different work–family investments or arrangements and apply to single employees without partners or children who still work, have families and personal lives outside of the workplace. Work and family can in fact be mutually reinforcing. And some employees can integrate or harmonise their work and family by choosing to keep them quite separate.

Organisational responses designed to address work–family concerns began with the development and articulation of work–family policies supportive of the family. These included such initiatives as flexible work hours, telecommuting, part-time work, childcare referrals, extended maternity benefits and paternal leaves. The evidence, however, showed these policy initiatives to be only moderately helpful in addressing work–family concerns. Work–family policies and programmes were often poorly communicated to employees. Some managers were minimally supportive of these policies and programmes. There was also the suspicion that employees using family-friendly policies and programmes were seen as lacking commitment to their organisations and were punished in subtle ways.

A more promising avenue to address work and family concerns seemed to lie in changing workplace cultures, structures and approaches to work and working. This is the subject of the present series of case studies organised by Suzan Lewis and Cary Cooper. This collection is unique in many ways. Other writers have described work–family best practices—those policies and programmes developed to address work–family concerns and how they might benefit employees and organisations. Some writers have also linked the presence and use of work–family policies and programmes with a limited set of personal and organisational outcomes, such as levels of work–family conflict and both work and family satisfaction. Lewis and Cooper emphasise, instead, the process of how organisations attempted to change their cultures and structures to be more supportive of work–family integration and the critical role of organisational learning in these efforts. Lewis and Cooper clearly lay out why organisations must change to better meet the needs of today's workforce.

These case studies highlight the different paths organisations have taken in grappling with work–family issues. Lewis and Cooper also distil some common principles of organisational change that are likely to apply to any organisation interested in experimenting and learning to become more supportive of work, family and personal well-being.

There are other insights offered in these case studies that are, on the one hand, interesting and useful to practice and, on the other hand, could be discouraging, especially for those who underestimate the complexity of organisational change and seek quick fixes. First, efforts to change organisational culture, structures and approaches to work and working are likely to require considerable resources and a long time frame. Second, the dual agenda approach, which emphasises both work performance and personal quality-of-life issues simultaneously, appears to hold much promise. Third, all the work–family experiments chronicled in these case studies have potential for further learning. Consistent with bringing about changes in any organisational process or system, bringing about successful changes in an organisation's culture and structure to support work–family harmonisation is a difficult undertaking, although the cases highlight the many potential benefits of doing so.

While many managers and professionals complain about work interfering with family, they choose to do nothing about it. In addition, employing organisations in industrialised countries continue to stress and reward task competencies over relationship competencies. Managers seem to be oblivious to new human resource management practices shown to meet both performance needs and employee well-being needs. It is not surprising that progress in addressing work and family has been slow. Fortunately, one can learn much from the change efforts described in this collection that were only partially successful. Lewis and Cooper distil change principles at the end of each case study that, if embraced, will increase the success rate of all future change efforts in this area.

Lewis and Cooper quite accurately place work and family issues as a societal concern. Many women and men in all industrialised countries experience work–personal life harmonisation difficulties and dissatisfaction. Although various countries have made different levels of progress and employed varied approaches, new thinking is needed here to move forward. This will, of necessity, involve challenging the priority of profits above people, the powerlessness that many individuals feel, the search for quick-fix solutions and the lack of collaboration among key stakeholders (e.g., governments, organisations, trade unions and professional associations, communities, families and individuals).

More people today want a life beyond work. Employees can work more effectively if they can integrate their work, families and personal lives in more satisfying ways. This becomes a win–win situation for all involved. This collection moves us in this direction.

Ronald J. Burke

Professor of Organizational Behavior
Schulich School of Business
York University
Canada

Foreword

by The Rt. Hon. Patricia Hewitt, MP

Work–life balance is a phrase that hardly causes business people to raise an eyebrow these days. Our best business leaders talk positively to their employees, to prospective staff and in public about the benefits they offer to their staff and, in turn, the flexibility that accrues to their business.

Yet the landscape of this debate has changed vastly from how it appeared just a decade ago. In 1993, when I wrote a book called *About Time*, setting out the challenges in the area of work and family life, the phrase "work–life balance" was not in the vocabulary of most business people—nor of most politicians! It was an aspect of our lives that public policy and our workplaces largely failed to address. What a contrast these days—now anyone who picks up a newspaper or magazine, or applies for a new job, is likely to be confronted by "flexible working" and work–life balance.

The authors have long championed the case for work–life balance and in this book they have looked in detail at which factors enable firms to implement work–life balance politics successfully. This is a helpful contribution as it also helps us to understand how best to introduce these into a workplace, and what might be the problem areas and how to get round them.

In Government, we have been promoting work–life balance and flexible working opportunities for some time now, demonstrating that there is a business case for work–life balance. In the future we want everyone to feel that they have more choice and control over their working lives. Flexible working opportunities benefit everyone: employers, employees and their families. Many employers tell us that it makes good business sense to provide flexible working opportunities for their staff. Using case studies, a body of research evidence, and a dedicated website, the DTI has highlighted the real business benefits reported to us by companies who have considered, and then implemented, alternative ways of working.

The business case for work–life balance for both employers and employees is clearly shown by the facts:

- 71% of employers who operate flexible working report that it has a positive impact on management–employee relations, employee motivation and commitment (69%), and labour turnover (54%).

- Almost half of employers report improvements in productivity, absenteeism and recruitment.

- There are also evident qualitative benefits for employers and their employees, chiefly improved morale and reduced levels of stress.

The DTI supports business and individuals interested in work–life balance in a number of ways. As well as raising awareness through advertising and the media, we have provided financial assistance to a number of projects in workplaces around the country, amounting to almost 450 employers with over a million employees between them. But our work continues—we are now promoting work–life balance as part of the overall way in which companies can become a high-performance workplace.

This book is a useful exploration of how organisations implement work–life balance policies. The Government has helped raise the awareness of businesses of the benefits of enabling staff to work in new ways enabling them to have more choice and control about their work. We will continue to explore ways of helping firms to discover the benefits of adopting good practice particularly when dealing with their most valuable resource, people.

The Rt. Hon. Patricia Hewitt, MP

November 2004

Acknowledgements

Many people have contributed to this book in important ways. In particular, Rhona Rapoport has been inspirational, as always. We are grateful for her clear-sighted, often challenging and always thought-provoking comments on earlier drafts of the book. Thanks go also to: Gill Carter, Jo Duff, Ian Greenaway, Jo Morris, Liz Raczi, Karen Silk, Ragnhild Sohlberg, Annamarie van Iren and Uracha Chatrakul Na Ayudhya for their insights and reflections on the case studies.

CHAPTER 1

Case Studies and Organisational Learning

How can organisations develop innovative working practices to adapt to and, more importantly, keep ahead of transformations in the workforce and in the nature of work? Specifically, how can they implement changes that enhance employees' opportunities to integrate their work and personal lives, and in so doing enhance workplace effectiveness in rapidly changing environments? These are the questions we explore in this book.

In this introductory chapter we first examine some of the reasons that organisations need to change to meet the needs of a diverse workforce in a rapidly shifting context and then explain how and why we use case studies to explore *processes of change* rather then just "good practice". We present some background to current debates on what is often called "work–life" balance and discuss the reasons we prefer to use the terms "work–personal life integration" or "work–personal life harmonisation". We then propose a model of organisational change to benefit workers and organisations that incorporates the role of organisational learning and perceptions of organisational justice. Some of the generic principles of change that emerge from the case studies are then discussed followed by an overview of the remainder of the book.

THE MISMATCH BETWEEN WORKING PRACTICES AND CURRENT REALITIES. WHY ORGANISATIONS NEED TO CHANGE

In most organisations there remains a mismatch between working practices on the one hand and current realities of the workforce and the nature of work in the "new" global economy on the other. First, traditional ways of working tend to overlook the diversity of the workforce. The percentage of women of working age in the labour force continues to grow (Hibbert & Meager, 2003) and few people have the backing of a full-time homemaker to enable them to work as though they have no other responsibilities or commitments. Growing numbers of men as well as women would like to work in ways that enable them to fulfil their potential at work while also leaving time and energy to spend with family or partake in other activities. For example, many young European workers talk about wanting to work in ways that they feel will allow them to "have a life" beyond work (Brannen, Lewis, Nilsen & Smithson, 2002; Lewis, Brannen & Smithson, 1999), and a study of chartered accountants in Britain revealed that even in this profession, which demands long and intense working hours, many younger accountants are resisting the work-dominated lifestyles of their seniors, asserting that they can work more effectively if they have the opportunity to integrate work and personal lives in more satisfying ways (Lewis, Cooper, Smithson & Dyer, 2003). Employers can benefit from the diverse set of experiences and perspectives of the contemporary workforce, who may question the logic of taken-for-granted working practices and provide insights into potentially more appropriate and innovative ways of doing things. Currently, however, these potential benefits tend to be constrained by workplace practices that assume that ideal employees have no responsibilities or interest beyond paid work or that there are no alternatives to current working practices and the long, inflexible and/or intense working hours to which they often lead (Rapoport, Bailyn, Fletcher & Pruitt, 2002).

Moreover, it is not just the composition of the workforce that is changing. The nature of jobs and of work itself is in flux. With global competition and the 24-hour marketplace, the growth of the knowledge economy and developments in information and communication technology, temporal and spatial boundaries between paid work and personal life have become increasingly blurred. People are experiencing an intensification of work in many different national and occupational contexts (Peper, Lewis & Den Dulk, 2004). They are working hard and often for long hours that intrude into personal time as technology ensures that many people are forever "on call". Jobs are also frequently experienced as insecure. It has been argued that global forces are calling for more and more effort in employment with very little consideration for the effect of this on people or societies (Rapoport, Lewis, Bailyn & Gambles, 2004) and that this is happening on a global scale, with tendencies, such as the extension and intensification of work, interacting with national culture (Brandth & Kvande, 2001, 2002; Poster, 2005) to produce working patterns that may be far from optimal for individuals, organisations and societies (Rapoport et al., 2004).

It is neither possible nor always desirable to hold back change. But, these forces for change could also be used in positive ways, to benefit organisations and their employees. For example, although not all the innovations described in this book relate to flexibility, those that do so focus on mutual flexibility and benefits. Flexibility of working time is often implemented to extend opening or operating times or increase production intensity and/or to prevent stress and burnout among those who are working longer and harder in more insecure jobs as a consequence of downsizing and restructuring. But, flexible working time arrangements based on high levels of trust and collaborative decision making can also benefit employees by providing the autonomy to fit in work and other activities. Similarly, information and communications technology facilitates hot-desking, working from home or other remote locations which can provide savings in office space and other benefits to organisations and can also, under some circumstances, enhance opportunities for employees to work in flexible ways and reduce commuting time. However, flexibility is an overarching term that incorporates a number of different types of organisational strategies including not only flexible working time and place arrangements but also functional, contractual, numerical, financial and geographical flexibility. The different forms of flexibility differ in the extent to which they solely benefit employers or are designed to meet the needs of both employers and employees. We focus in this book on organisational changes, relating to flexibility or other ways of restructuring work, that can contribute towards mutual benefits to employers and employees.

Although some of the changes introduced in some of the case studies are about flexible working arrangements, others go beyond this with such changes as multi-skilling or self-managing teams. Some introduce innovations in the ways in which people engage with each other at work, such as by the reorganisation of time to minimise unnecessary interruptions, different ways of managers engaging with staff on long-term sick leave, different ways of engaging with suppliers or proposed different ways of engaging with clients.

The business case for considering work–personal life issues when implementing change is now widely argued, by researchers and also by employers with positive experiences of changes with win–win outcomes (Bevan, Dench, Tamkin & Cummings, 1999; DTI, 2001; Lewis, Cooper et al., 2003). Sometimes, there is more of a focus on the business outcomes than personal outcomes (or, indeed, vice versa), but we argue that ideally the two should be treated as equally important. This is one of the findings of a programme of action research (specifically, collaborative interactive action research) developed in the USA by Rhona Rapoport, Lotte Bailyn and their colleagues, that focuses on the way work is done and links the goal of increasing gender equity and work–personal life integration to the goal of improved workplace performance in what they term a "Dual Agenda" (Rapoport et al., 2002, p. 18). This is discussed in more detail in Chapter 2. Though most of our cases do not explicitly use this approach, they do illustrate the effectiveness of taking account of both employee and organisational needs in developing sustainable and equitable workplace change. Such change always involves going beyond the development of policy to actual practice. The goal is systemic change—that is, changes in workplace structures, cultures and practices—embedded in organisational learning and perceived as equitable by all involved.

It would be absurd to think that working practices that may have been appropriate in industrial times with predominantly male workforces can be transferred with no more than a little tweaking to meet the radically changed needs of diverse, post-industrial institutions in the global and technological era. All organisations have to learn and adapt to changes that are all around them—but, some do so faster and more effectively than others. These may be described as "learning organisations"—that is, organisations in which people are collectively and continually expanding their knowledge to create their future (Senge, 1990). Work–

personal life integration issues are a significant part of the context that has to be taken into account in creating this learning.

WHY CASE STUDIES?

Case studies can be a useful source of organisational learning. They can be used to describe interventions in specific organisational contexts, illustrate principles and processes of change and explore the reasons for particular outcomes. However, in the field of work–personal life integration, case studies are often presented as examples of good practice. That is, it is the outcomes and not the process that is described. Sometimes, this is superficial; for example, policies are described but not the extent to which they are implemented in practice nor the impact on the wider organisation. Organisation-level change may be minimal (there may, for example, be policies offering opportunities for flexibility that are rarely taken up), or it may be substantial, involving real shifts in culture and practice. But, wider organisational change and, importantly, the processes by which it may be achieved are rarely discussed in detail. Good practice examples are good for a company's PR and can inspire others to develop change programmes; but, without an in-depth analysis of processes, they are often of limited benefit as a guide to change. There are a number of reasons for this.

First, good practices cannot be generalised, although as discussed on p. 12 there are generic *principles* of change. What is good practice for one particular work group in one organisation may not be appropriate in other contexts. Every organisation (or in large firms, parts of the organisation) is different in some ways. What we can usefully learn from positive experiences of change is about the process of getting there. It is the generic principles of change rather than resulting practices that have wider currency. Second, even when desirable changes are achieved, there is never room for complacency— workplaces and their contexts are constantly changing and there is a need for continuous learning. Today's good practice in a specific context may be inadequate tomorrow, which is why an understanding of process is more useful than just practices for sustaining long-term positive outcomes. And, third, good practice case studies tend to focus on success stories while glossing over failures experienced and barriers overcome in the process.

This limits opportunities for diffusing learning both internally—for example, across departments—and externally. Much of the learning that takes place from successful initiatives comes from the experience of going through a process of change, which will inevitably involve some risk and failures and barriers. We can often learn as much from failures as successes.

Our intention therefore is not to duplicate the many examples of "good practice" that are available (see, for example, the DTI website *www.DTI.gov.uk*), but rather to explore in more depth the processes whereby a small number of selected organisations learn (to various extents) that practices which support the work–personal life integration of their workforce also contribute to organisational effectiveness, and, in most of the examples, implement structural and cultural changes on that basis.

We have chosen seven case studies to demonstrate the process of change through a focus on work–personal life, as well as some other brief examples (see Boxes 9.1 and 9.2 on pp. 121 and 124–125). We begin with a classic case study (Xerox, see Chapter 2) illustrating a particular approach: collaborative interactive action research in the United States (see Rapoport et al., 2002), which has been influential in many other countries. In two of the case studies reported here we, the authors, were directly involved as researchers (Proffirm and Recruitco). We also interviewed change agents in a range of organisations that had achieved some measure of change to support employees and employers, focusing on the change process (see Appendix A for the interview guide) and in some cases also talked to some employees. From these interviews we selected a further four organisations to illustrate different presenting problems driving change, organisational characteristics, processes of change and stage of organisational learning. We have included international cases because this is important in a global context and for wider learning, as few organisations operate totally independently from these broader issues. Size of organisation is also important. Larger organisations often have a range of formal policies, but these tend to have limited impact in practice (Lewis, Cooper et al., 2003). Smaller organisations tend to have fewer formal policies, but in some cases can have more informal flexibility. We have included two smaller organisations. One in which the changes were introduced to avoid possible bankruptcy and involved total transformation of working practices. In the other there was a history of flexibility and management supportiveness, promoted by the chief executive so it was difficult to understand why this was not bringing about the desired changes, until external researchers stimulated the change process. Most of the larger organisations had work–life policies in place, though they varied in the extent to which the culture was supportive of those who sought to take up entitlements. However, formal policies and supportive managers were not sufficient to generate the full possible benefits of innovative ways of working to the organisation or to employees.

We have not systematically collected data from employees about their experiences of outcomes because our focus is on process, although most organisations have carried out workforce surveys as part of their evaluation of changes. If employees were to be interviewed there would inevitably be pockets of discontent despite the positive outcomes of these surveys. Such pockets of discontent could be regarded as possible levers for future change using the processes described. Change is inevitably an ongoing process as neither internal nor external context stands still. These cases we have selected do not of course cover all the possible different contexts. There are many examples of organisations that are working towards fundamental change to meet the dual agenda of enhancing organisational effectiveness and opportunities for satisfying and equitable integration of work and personal life.

From p. 12 we develop some principles of change to guide managers, human resource professionals and others seeking to achieve organisational success through enhancing opportunities for members of the workforce to harmonise their work and personal life, making optimum contributions to both. First, however, it is important to look at the background to research and debates on organisational change and the relationship between employment and personal life, and the terminology used to frame the issues. Although many people regard "work–life balance" issues as something new, in contemporary society they have been around for quite some time.

DEVELOPMENTS IN RESEARCH AND DEBATE ON WORK–PERSONAL LIFE INTEGRATION AND ORGANISATIONAL CHANGE—AND IMPLICATIONS FOR PRACTICE

Terminology: How We Talk About the Issues

Work–personal life issues and especially work–life balance have become hot topics in recent government and employer discussions, among human resource professionals and consultants, in the media and in everyday language. But, "work–life balance" is a problematic term. We prefer to talk about work–personal life integration or harmonisation. The phrase "work–life balance" seems to suggest that work is not a part of life, although for many people work is increasingly dominating their lives. Furthermore, the word "balance" seems to imply a trade-off—one side goes up, the other goes down—yet work and personal life are not necessarily antithetical or mutually exclusive, but can be mutually reinforcing. For example, skills learned in personal life can enhance effectiveness in work life and vice versa. Finally, work–life balance suggests the possibility of a quick fix—just tip the scales a bit. In this book we emphasise that quick fixes do not provide sustainable long-term solutions.

The term "work–personal life integration" was introduced to address some of these difficulties (e.g., Parasuraman & Greenhaus, 1997; Lewis, Rapoport et al., 2003; Rapoport et al., 2004). This was to denote an ideal of being able to integrate paid work and personal lives rather than seeing them as two separate (and by implication incompatible) areas of life that have to be "balanced" and to capture the potential synergies and connections between many different parts of life (see Lewis, Rapoport & Gambles, 2003; Rapoport et al., 2002). Nevertheless, the terminology used remains contentious. One misunderstanding of the term "integration" is that it implies work and personal life must be integrated in the sense of merging into each other, ruling out the strategy of integrating the two by deliberately keeping these domains separate. This was not the intention. Consequently, the word "harmonisation" has been introduced as an attempt to get over this problem and to indicate an aim of relating work and personal life domains in positive or harmonious ways (see Gambles, Lewis & Rapoport, forthcoming, and also Appendix B).[1] In this book we use "work–personal life harmonisation" or "work–personal life integration" interchangeably.[2]

History of the Debates

Whatever the terminology used, however, the debate about how to succeed in occupational life without sacrificing personal life has grown out of a long tradition of research and discussion relating to the interface between work and family or personal life. Looking back, research on work–family or work–life issues began in the mid-1960s (Rapoport & Rapoport, 1965) and developed from a tendency to focus on women, work–family conflict and stress to a more recent focus on all employees, and on the question of how to achieve positive work–personal life integration and organisational as well as individual well-being. Early organisational responses focused on family-friendly or work–life policies, such as flexitime, part-time or reduced hours working and childcare assistance or support with eldercare. Formal workplace policies alone, however, turned out to be of limited value (Hochschild, 1997; Lewis, 1997, 2001). Often they were (and in some cases still are) poorly communicated within organisations and take-up tends to be low. Many of those employees who most needed flexibility were unaware of policies and entitlements (Lewis, Kagan & Heaton, 2000). In some cases this was a deliberate strategy, because flexibility was regarded as a favour rather than as a strategic tool to enhance effectiveness and there was concern to limit the number of people who "took advantage" of opportunities to work in different ways. Above all, these initiatives tended to be regarded as policies for women, or at least for those who could not or did not wish to conform to standard working times, regarded as the ideal, and subsequently were marginalized as non-ideal workers. Take-up of formal family-friendly policies continues to be regarded by employees and employers as career-limiting in many

[1] The use of the term "harmonisation" emerged from reflections on a study of work and personal life issues in seven countries, *Work–personal Life Integration: Looking Backwards to Go Forwards*. This was funded by a grant from the Ford Foundation to the Institute of Family and Environmental Research for work involving Rhona Rapoport, Suzan Lewis and Richenda Gambles. See also Appendix B.
[2] Another term, favoured in Europe, is the "reconciliation of family life and employment", but our focus here goes beyond family life to other non-work arenas of life.

contexts (Lewis, Cooper et al., 2003). They enable those with family commitments to retain links with employment but limit opportunities for advancement in organisations.

It is now increasingly accepted that formal policies may be an essential first step in larger organisations (often informal flexibility is available and effective in smaller organisations), but are not sufficient to bring about real change in working practices (Lewis, 1997, 2001; Lewis, Rapoport et al., 2003; Rapoport et al., 2002). More fundamental structural and cultural changes are necessary if organisations and employees are to derive the full benefits from work–personal life initiatives through a dual agenda approach. Cultural and structural change takes longer than policy implementation, but there is evidence that it can happen, saving time in the long term and with real bottom-line benefits (Rapoport et al., 2002).

Work–life or work–family concerns as they were initially known were originally considered within equal opportunities programmes, with a particular focus on women, especially mothers. However, increasing evidence that men as well as women, with and without children, want time for a personal life, together with growing evidence of a strong business case for addressing work–life issues have brought this out of the equal opportunities arena into the sphere of diversity management. Responding to work–life issues is increasingly viewed as a strategic business concern in the most forward-looking organisations. Other organisations, however, take a more short-term view of the "business case" for change, and the introduction of token work–life policies with immediate short-term benefits, such as enhanced retention, can detract from the need to look more deeply at actual working practices and inherent assumptions that sustain counterproductive behaviours and values. A focus on the ways in which change occurs and the time this takes is often ignored. The desire for quick fixes or "best practice" policies often results in a failure to ask tricky questions about conflicting values or to challenge deeply entrenched—but outdated—assumptions and practices, such as the overvaluing of visible time at the workplace and subsequent lack of flexibility of working time and place. There are no easy or quick fixes and no "one size fits all" solutions.

The search for quick fixes is understandable when so many people are experiencing the time squeeze with intense workloads and a sense of being perpetually busy (Bunting, 2004). It is often difficult to find the time to think more deeply about the long-terms goals of work–personal life initiatives and processes for working towards them. So, the solutions proposed are often superficial; for example, implementing a flexitime system from the top, without collaborating with staff to ensure it meets everyone's needs and without addressing a culture which values only those working non-flexible hours. Such an approach will have limited impact and, though apparently less time-consuming than the process we advocate here, it will ultimately mean time wasted. Spending a little more time to get the changes right will have more long-term pay-offs.

Along with changes in workplace policies there have also been important developments in public policies, particularly in Europe. These include entitlements to parental leave and leave to deal with family emergencies, paid in some countries, rights for part-time workers, regulations of working time and, in the UK, the right to ask for flexible working arrangements which employers are required to consider. However, although public policies provide essential entitlements and oblige employers to adapt at least to some extent, these policies still have to be implemented at the workplace level. This will remain problematic as long as the benefits to organisations as well as employees are not apparent. Meanwhile, informal norms, such as a long-hours culture or lack of trust in people to work flexibly, can and does undermine these policies. For example, in Norway and Sweden where progressive policy includes long paid parental leave, one month of which has to be taken by the father and cannot be transferred to the mother, there has been a substantial increase in the number of fathers taking this leave. Nevertheless, there remain "greedy" organisations which make it difficult for men to take up these entitlements in practice, or even to eschew long hours, without damaging their careers, a situation that is exacerbated in the context of global competition (Brandth & Kvande, 2001, 2002; Haas & Hwang, 1995).

LEEDS METROPOLITAN UNIVERSITY LIBRARY

Basic organisational structures, cultures and practices have not yet been widely challenged by legislative and workplace policies. For example, assumptions about what it means to be a "committed" or "competent" employee, which often incorporate a view that these ideal workers do not adapt their work to fit in family or other commitments, have rarely been thought through. Why is it assumed that people who neglect their families make better workers, that being a good worker and having other commitments are incompatible, or that the skills learnt in, for example, parenting are of no value in the workplace? *The case studies in this book illustrate the importance of going beyond policy gestures to embark on a process which first challenges assumptions that sustain outdated practices and then draws on collaboration to develop more appropriate and effective norms and practices.*

PROCESSES AND PRINCIPLES OF CHANGE

This book will focus on the processes of change in workplaces— systemic change that is change in culture, structures and practices— not just policies. We have insisted on anonymity for the organisations (except in one case that has been reported elsewhere, see Chapter 2) to ensure that we can communicate total learning experiences. But, all the organisations have been brave enough to take the initial risks necessary to achieve fundamental change and not just playing around at the margins—and have benefited from doing so, albeit to different extents depending on the stage of learning achieved.

Change is taking place all the time in organisations and in their local, national and global contexts. So, managing change is a key strategic challenge for organisations. It is possible to manage change by reacting and adapting to it. Or organisations can create and lead change, to which others can react. Harnessing the creativity released when employees can collaborate to problem-solve on the basis of a dual agenda of both organisational needs and their own work–personal life integration needs is one way of anticipating and leading rather than reacting to or worse still ignoring change (Rapoport et al., 2002).

Although there are no best practices that can be widely applied, there are principles and processes that can be adapted across a wide range of contexts. As a vice-president of Energyco (see Chapter 3) told us:

> *I have travelled around talking to managers in many different countries. It is surprising how the issues and problems relating to the integration of work and personal life are converging. And I find that the principles and processes of successful solutions are similar though the practicalities differ according to context, including national and regulatory contexts and type*

of organisation. Less successful solutions are, for example, those which target only women and add men as an afterthought or which focus on policies only for parents.

(From an interview with a change agent—Energyco)

It is these principles and processes and their contribution to organisational learning that we will be exploring in this book.

ORGANISATIONAL LEARNING

The most successful change initiatives in relation to work–personal life integration, as in other organisational areas, always involves an element of *organisational learning*. Too often work–personal life integration issues are articulated as individual concerns. HR or line managers explore ways in which individual employees can be supported in managing their work and personal lives—particularly women with young children. However well-meaning this approach, a failure to look at wider organisational values and practices reduces opportunities for organisational learning and employees and employers lose out.

Organisational learning involves a process of gaining knowledge and developing skills which empower people to understand and consequently to act effectively within organisations. It enhances capacity for effective action (Senge et al., 1999). The most powerful organisational learning comes from direct experience—learning by doing (Nonaka & Takeuchi, 1995; Barnett, 1994; Rapoport et al., 2002). Thus, organisational learning is an experience-based process that changes the collective state of knowledge (including assumptions) in organisations. Through this process knowledge about the relationships between action and outcomes develops and this is built into routines and becomes embedded in organisational memory, changing collective behaviour (Barnett, 1994).

The notion of organisational learning assumes that collectives of people that make up the organisation can learn from past experience and transform experiences into new knowledge. Although the focus is on learning at the organisational level, learning begins with individuals. However, the structures in which most people work nowadays, and particularly the intensification of work and the time squeeze, are often not conducive to reflection and engagement (Senge, 1990), so it is important to provide opportunities for reflective thinking for systemic change to take place. But, organisational leaning takes place not just by the sum of individuals' learning but also through social interactions and depends on processes of negotiation and consensus-making. Collaboration and interaction are crucial to the process (Rapoport et al., 2002).

Organisational learning can produce systemic change and development. This approach recognises that organisations are complex systems. Focusing on just one part of the system (e.g., working hours) without seeing how it relates to the whole organisation can mean that decision makers never see the full consequences of their actions or decisions. Thus, when faced with a problem, decisions are often made which are seen to be capable of improving the situation in a relatively short time. For example, opening a workplace nursery or otherwise assisting with childcare can enhance recruitment and retention and enable parents to work, but leave the basic workplace culture and structures, such as the norm of long working hours and holding meetings out of working hours, unchanged if it is not accompanied by some rethinking of working time.

Moreover, when viewed in systems terms initiatives with short-term benefits can often have long-term costs. For example, downsizing the workforce to deal with financial problems in a recession can have immediate short-term benefits to the budget, but may have detrimental long-term effects if the organisation does not have the human capital to respond to a rise in demand when the economy improves. Similarly, permitting individual workers to work part-time, while continuing to see full-time workers as more valuable can have the short-term effect of improving retention, but, in the absence of wider organisational change, the long-term effect will be to perpetuate the overvaluing of full-time inflexible workers and the inability to respond flexibly to future demands.

The short-term responses involve survival or adaptive learning (Senge, 1990). This type of learning is necessary, but the learning organisation also needs generative or transformational learning, that takes account of complex systems and long-term outcomes, to enhance capacity to excel (Senge, 1990).

Senge et al. (1999) describe the organisational learning process in terms of exploring and learning from new possibilities, often via pilot projects, which provide experiential learning, which can then be diffused more widely across the organisation, creating capacity for collective action. Most of the cases discussed in this book used pilot projects. At other times the process involves learning from possibilities that present themselves; for example, from bottom-up initiatives or trends for more people to want to work flexibly or reduced hours. These can be viewed as opportunities to experiment with new ways of working. Often, the same opportunities for learning are presented to many organisations, but only some are ready to really transform experience into new knowledge. In this book Energyco is an example of an organisation that was able to learn from opportunities presented by bottom-up initiatives for using technology to enhance flexibility of working time and place, while (Printco) learnt from challenges faced when responding to a dire financial situation.

Differences in readiness to learn from opportunities presented by requests for flexible working are illustrated by Lee, MacDermid and Buck (2000) who studied companies in which managers and professionals had requested and been given opportunities to work less than full time, to see how employers learned from this. This was a qualitative study, which involved interviews with 82 managers or professionals working less than full time in 42 different organisations. For each of the managers or professionals interviewed the researchers also interviewed their managers, a co-worker, a human resources representative and the manager/professional's spouse or partner, to generate multiple perspectives on the impacts of reduced hours work. Three different paradigms of reduced hours' working emerged, illustrating different approaches to organisational learning: accommodation, elaboration and transformation.

Lee et al. (2000) used the term "accommodation" to apply to organisations making minimal adjustments in response to permitting managers or professionals to work less than full time. Often, people working reduced hours are more efficient than full timers, but if the organisation is steeped in the assumption that only full-time workers are good employees this is unlikely to be recognised and therefore fail to contribute to organisational learning. Lee et al. (2000) found that in organisations characterised by accommodation there was a view that only certain jobs were suitable to be performed in reduced hours or that only certain exceptional individuals could manage this. Employers accommodated requests for reduced hours reluctantly, usually to retain a highly valued manager, but this was still largely regarded as a career-limiting move by the individuals and their managers. Employers were concerned to contain and limit this different way of working so that others would not think they could follow suit. There was little or no organisational learning. So, responding to requests for flexible working from a few exceptional people, without learning about the wider benefits of implementing wider change, is accommodation. We have not included any case studies of organisations at the stage of accommodation in this book, although they may be described elsewhere as displaying good practice.

A second form of organisational learning described by Lee et al. (2000) was elaboration which occurred in organisations where there were formal policies supporting alternative ways of working and a prevailing view that these would benefit the organisation as well as individual employees—for example, by reducing turnover. Alternative ways of working were seen as part of a trend as a response to diversity. There were mixed views about how this would affect individual careers, but it was assumed that full timers would still be at an advantage in this respect. The employer's response was to control and systemize procedures for alternative ways of working. So, there was some learning, but it was limited by assumptions about trust and the need to have formal procedures in place. Several of the case study organisations discussed in this book are at the elaboration stage. They have undergone organisational learning and are on the way to, but have not yet achieved, transformation.

Transformation implies a greater willingness to embrace change and learn from opportunities presented by employees working less than full time. In the Lee et al. (2000) study of professionals and managers, reduced load working was accepted whether or not there were formal policies in place. This was viewed as a normal reaction to the need to retain good people and an opportunity to learn about how to be more flexible in changing contexts. The focus was not on hours worked by managers but on, for example, developing the best people and preparing them for future leadership roles in the long term. The employer stance was not to limit or formalise, but to experiment and learn. Several of the case study organisations discussed in this book have achieved transformation either throughout the organisation, or in larger organisations, in some departments or work groups.

New legislation in Britain giving employees the right to request flexible working and obliging employers to consider these requests unless there are good operational reasons to refuse, will provide more organisations with opportunities to learn. Employers' responses and the benefits that they derive will depend on their openness to organisational learning.

In this book we examine cases where organisations pursue a goal of transformational learning that goes beyond adapting to the needs of specific individuals to find broader win–win solutions which have organisation-wide implications and benefits. Not all have achieved these goals yet, but all have at least begun the process.

ORGANISATIONAL JUSTICE

People in organisations are most likely to be committed to change initiatives of any kind if they perceive the changes as fair and equitable. Often so-called work–life balance initiatives are not perceived as equitable, but are thought to benefit some people (e.g., parents of young children) more than others, often resulting in resentment or backlash (Young, 1999; Lewis, 2002).

Judgements about whether changes, including work–personal life policies and practices are fair, tend to vary according to perceptions of the fairness of outcomes (distributive justice), perceived fairness of processes (procedural justice—e.g., if work teams collaborated in the development of new initiatives) and management sensitivity and support in administering procedures (interpersonal justice). The more equitable outcomes are perceived to be, the more satisfied those involved feel, while outcomes perceived as unfair generate dissatisfaction (Folger & Kanovsky, 1989). So, for example, backlash can occur if employees without immediate caring responsibilities feel they are expected to do more work to cover for others. This perceived distributive injustice may be compounded by perceived procedural injustice if workers are not consulted, or better still collaborated with, on policy and practice changes or if managers are perceived as showing favouritism. The more workers feel they have been involved in decision making and contributed to equitable solutions the more committed they will be to these decisions. The impact of perceptions of justice are illustrated in several of the case studies in this book. For example, Chapter 6 describes a company (Recruitco) in which there is a culture of support and empowerment, and yet informal flexibility, designed to empower employees, was perceived as unfair because of the way that it was implemented in practice. A new system designed collaboratively with employees enhanced perceptions of distributive, procedural and interpersonal justice.

One form of justice of particular relevance to work–personal life issues is gender justice. This is discussed further in Chapter 2, with evidence that gender-equitable working practices are associated with workplace effectiveness while gendered assumptions undermine both gender equity and organisational effectiveness (Rapoport et al., 2002).

MODEL OF CHANGE

When thinking about organisational change we have to begin with the questions what, why, who and how? In the case studies in this book, *what* the desired changes are includes systemic change based on a re-thinking of workplace norms, values and practices to achieve win–win solutions. With the exception of one of the cases in this book, which did not result in substantial change for reasons that we will discuss, all the other case studies involve a shift towards greater innovation in working arrangements. There are also other changes, linked to the specific needs and characteristics of the case study organisation.

The reasons *why* such change is necessary are because of changes in the nature of the workforce, in the nature of work and in the global context. We might also consider the social consequences, for families and communities of working practices, which undermine work–personal life integration (Lewis, Rapoport et al., 2003). We return to this point in

Chapter 9. For organisations to be motivated to change, however, there has to be recognition of a specific business-related problem. Problems faced by the case study organisations include, for example, high staff turnover, the need to recruit and retain the most talented employees to compete globally, or lack of profitability (see Boxes 1.1–1.5 on pp. 22–24).

Who are the change agents? In some cases change agents are external or new to the organisation. These include collaborative interactive action researchers (Xerox) or researchers using some aspects of an action research approach (Proffirm). In one case it is a new managing director who transforms the organisation (Printco) while Box 1.1 (see p. 22) highlights a role for trade unions. External or new people do not take for granted assumptions, norms and everyday working practices and so are able to ask questions that may not occur to those well-socialised into the organisation. However, they are also not in the power structure of the organisation, which can be a problem when attempts are made to diffuse the process of change more widely. It also makes a difference whether external change agents are funded by the organisation or by an external body, such as a research funder (see Xerox, Proffirm) or government (see Recruitco and Box 1.2 on pp. 22 and 23). External change agents not funded by the organisation tend to have more independence and to be less influenced by organisational agendas that might undermine appropriate changes.

In another case (Energyco) the change agents can be described as the workers themselves, although senior management were ready to build upon bottom-up initiatives to generate transformational learning in some parts of the company, albeit not yet company-wide. Often, change is led by HR. If HR is powerful (e.g., if there is an HR director on the board), this may be useful. But, often the change agent in HR lacks position power and is perceived as pursuing people issues rather than both people and strategic business issues. This was the case in Adminco, where despite using a process with potential to lead to innovation the HR manager's lack of knowledge about strategic plans also undermined the process.

How is change brought about? All the case studies start with the recognition of a specific problem and acknowledgment that work–life policies alone are not sufficient to bring about real change to meet the dual agenda of work–personal life integration and enhanced effectiveness. There are no quick fixes for sustainable and equitable change. Change is ongoing and iterative. Some generic principals emerge from these case studies, including the need to listen, reflect and bring to the surface assumptions, the importance of participation and collaboration of those affected by any changes, experimenting with job redesign, working with resisting, experiencing and diffusing the process of change. Some of these are discussed in more detail below.

Action-oriented research

Action research in organisations is defined by Eden and Huxham (1999) as research that results from an involvement by a researcher or re-searchers with members of an organisation and relates to a matter which is of genuine concern, in which there is an intent by organisa-tional members to take action based on the intervention. One specific form of action research, based on a dual agenda is used in the Xerox case study and others use elements of action research. However, using the word "research" in the wider sense of examining evidence about working practices, the reasons that they are sustained and their implica-tions, with a commitment to change in order to address organisational concerns, all the processes described in the case studies could all be designated as a form of action-oriented research. Action-oriented research differs from consultancy in that it is a process of enquiry in which there is mutual learning whereas consultancy implies that solutions to problems are provided by experts.

Collaboration

Successful change initiatives tend to be based on collaboration between members of a work group, including managers and change agents (re-searcher, consultant, CEO, HR manager). Some change initiatives are based on consultation rather than collaboration. This involves finding out about employees' needs and then feeding them into the decision-making process in some way, but not involving the workforce directly in decision making. Collaboration, on the other hand, involves all stakeholders in a particular decision working together to understand problems and find solutions to particular issues. The views and experiences of job holders as well as those who manage them are crucial to creative and workable decisions about how work could be done differently in specific jobs.

A collaborative model of change implies a participatory approach to research, with an equalising of power between researchers and other participants. In their collaborative interactive action research approach, Rapoport et al. also talk about fluid expertise; that is, a mode of working together that respects the skills and knowledge that each person brings to the collaboration and allows expertise to shift from one to another depending on the needs of the situation (Rapoport et al., 2002, p. 67). Although not explicitly articulated in other case studies this approach is sometimes used (e.g., in Printco). Collaboration can generate innovative ideas grounded in practice and experience. It also helps to ensure that all have a stake in and are therefore committed to make innovative interventions work.

Resistance

There is always resistance to change. Resistance can be conceived as something negative that has to be overcome. But, it can also be understood as a positive force for change, or as a motor for change as in various political forms of resistance. The approach taken by Rapoport et al. (2002) and discussed in Chapter 2 is to treat resistance as useful and important providing valuable data which it is important to incorporate into any analysis of the work context and its requirements. It is a sign of where tension exists that can be worked with to bring about change. Rapoport et al. (2002) aim to challenge underlying assumptions about working practices in order to move resistance from a desire to block constructive changes towards resistance against current systems that undermine work–personal life integration and workplace effectiveness. Resistance is usually found among workers or managers, but other forms of resistance emerge in the case studies including, for example, resistance from unions (Energyco). In some of the case studies, resistance is perceived as, and consequently turns out to be, a stumbling block to further progress.

A MODEL AND PRINCIPLES OF CHANGE TO GUIDE MANAGERS, HUMAN RESOURCE PROFESSIONALS AND CONSULTANTS SEEKING TO ACHIEVE ORGANISATIONAL SUCCESS THROUGH ENHANCING WORK–LIFE INTEGRATION

Box 1.1

Presenting problem or issue—i.e., salient business needs that are evident at the outset (others may emerge in the process):

- Need to recruit and retain the most talented employees to compete globally in a knowledge economy.
- Financial problems.
- High turnover.
- Gender inequities.
- A need to reduce time-to-market problems in getting collaboration between different departments.
- Lack of trust and flexibility.
- High absenteeism.
- Backlash against people who use work–life policy entitlements.
- Lack of flexibility and adaptability.
- Resistance to new ways of working (e.g., self-managed teams).

⬇

Box 1.2

Process includes:

- Pilot projects working with work units.
- Often involves an external change agent.
- Support from the top is essential.
- Looking at working practices through a work–personal life lens.
- Pursuing a dual agenda of work–personal life integration (or gender equity) and workplace effectiveness—always keeping the two in mind.
- Surface and challenge assumptions underpinning working practices that undermine the dual agenda.

- Apply this to the salient business needs addressed at the outset or emerging during the process.
- Listening, reflection and mutual learning.
- Collaborative and creative thinking to address problems and consider appropriate job redesign.
- Work with all stakeholders, including senior management, work teams and union or other worker representatives.
- Work with resistance as a positive force.
- Pilot solutions (new ways of working) suspending judgement for a set period of time, and evaluate.
- Diffuse the learning more widely within the organisation.

Box 1.3

Intervening factors:

- Organisational learning.
- Perceived justice and fairness.
- Gender equity.

Box 1.4

Some solutions (based on the specific needs of each organisation and feasible because of the process by which initiatives are developed):

- Flexibility is open to all; and is two-way. Usually informal but may need to be formal for a while.
- Self-managed teams—arranging their own cover.
- Better time management across the work unit or organisation.
- Multi-skilling.
- A new language of flexibility encouraging future innovations.

Box 1.5

Outcomes can include:

- Increased profitability.
- Reduction in sickness absence.
- Reduced staff turnover.

- Shortened time to market.
- Increased employee satisfaction.
- Increased customer satisfaction.
- Extended cover of services, opening hours or use of equipment.
- Avoidance of deadline crises; therefore, better service, more effective working and less pressure.
- Increased worker creativity and innovation and general effectiveness.
- Increased sales.
- Increased ability to adapt to new circumstances including changes in markets and in legislation.
- Enhanced recruitment and retention. Perceived as a good place to work.
- Better use of office space.
- Culture change—higher trust and better morale.
- Better team relationships—no backlash against those using work–life policies.
- Enhanced opportunities for the harmonisation of work and personal life and for gender equity.

OVERVIEW OF THE BOOK

Chapter 2 sets out a case study that is a now-classic example of how a particular form of action research (collaborative interactive action research) can be used to meet a dual agenda of work–personal life integration and enhanced workplace effectiveness in work units within one organisation (the Xerox Corporation). Transformational learning was achieved in units where the collaborative process and subsequent interventions were experienced, but there was no opportunity to diffuse learning across the company. The theory and process described in Chapter 2 inform our analysis of the other case studies in subsequent chapters. Although most do not use action research, and none specific-ally use all aspects of the collaborative interactive action research approach, they do incorporate some elements of this process, explicitly or implicitly, and illustrate some of the principles emerging from the Xerox case.

Chapter 3 is a case study of a large multinational company with a culture of empowerment and minimal central control, which was able to respond to and learn from bottom-up initiatives for increased flexibility of working arrangements to benefit the organisation and its employees. We describe the process of transformational learning in some areas of the organisation, but show that learning was uneven across the organisation and there is a need for ongoing learning to anticipate or manage new challenges. The study demonstrates how systemic change can be achieved in some parts of an organisation, but shows that if this is not diffused to become organisation-wide it can create new problems.

Chapter 4 discusses a case in which the first stages of a collaborative action research process were carried out, leading to the identification of a number of counterproductive working practices and the assumptions that underpinned them. It was clear that these were restricting both effectiveness and work–personal life integration of the workforce. However, the surfacing of these assumptions and some collaborative thinking about how to challenge them was not sufficient as there was no agreement that there were business problems and therefore little commitment among senior management to take action to bring about change. There was a reluctance to experiment by implementing the possible interventions that were beginning to emerge from collaborative thinking. The change process takes time, but short-term approaches to time emerged as a major theme in this organisation and an issue permeating the whole process. We reflect on the reasons it was not possible to take forward the organisational learning gained from the early stages of the process to bring about transformative changes in practices and culture.

Chapter 5 is an example of organisational change to support business effectiveness and employee work–personal life integration in a small business. It is often argued that small businesses cannot undertake change to support work–personal life integration because there is less scope for covering flexible workers and fewer resources. This case suggests that there may in fact be more scope for change in a small organisation, where the whole workplace may be the unit of change with less need for pilot studies and for wider diffusion than in larger organisations. This case illustrates how total flexibility based on high levels of trust and reciprocity, where flexibility is regarded as a strategic opportunity to innovate rather than a system that must be formalised and limited, has the power to not only support work–personal life integration but also to transform a struggling business into a thriving concern.

Not all the case studies deal with organisations that have had a complete turnaround of culture. Recruitco, the subject of Chapter 6, is another small company. In this case the chief executive has always understood the dual agenda and the importance of empowering and treating her staff well. Yet, attempts to introduce informal flexible-working arrangements had run into difficulties. This case study illustrates that support from the top is not sufficient and explores the process whereby a small business that already recognised the importance of work–personal life integration was able to develop its working practices systematically, to meet the needs of both employees and the business in a way that is experienced as equitable.

The process described in the case study in Chapter 7 has much in common with those of the other chapters, but also differs in notable ways. The change process is developed by a champion in HR with few resources, pursuing a business agenda for flexible working emanating from management. Starting from a base of highly traditional ways of working with no flexibility, he eschewed the most usual HR approach of developing policies and focused instead on a change process embodying many of the principles illustrated in the other case studies. A considerable measure of success was achieved in two of the pilot projects, with many desired business outcomes, and we reflect on the reasons for the failure of the third pilot project. Flexibility remains rather formal and constrained at this stage, but the journey towards transformation is ongoing. The complexities of this case offer many insights and learning points.

Chapter 8 provides a unique case of a charitable organisation, Charityco, which provides services for learning for disabled children and adults. It has a staff of over 50 who provide 24-hour care, 365 days a year. With the majority of staff being women who have some degree of childcare responsibility, the difficulty of maintaining work–life balance or coping with work–personal issues is a fundamental problem. The chief executive of Charityco provides her perspective on the issues and how she tackled them.

In each chapter we introduce the organisation and the issues they faced before the change process began, identify some of the traditional assumptions challenged in the case study, describe the process of change and summarise the main learning points. We also point to the outcomes which in every case where change was achieved extended well beyond supporting employees in the integration of their work and personal life. The benefits to the organisations are many, substantial and often quite surprising.

Chapter 9 reflects on some of the deeper issues that go beyond the dual agenda of work–personal life integration and workplace effectiveness to propose a multiple agenda that also addresses some of the wider social consequences of many of the current ways of working in the contemporary global context.

CHAPTER 2

The Xerox Corporation

A classic case study using collaborative interactive action research (CIAR) with a dual agenda of enhanced opportunities for work–personal life integration and enhanced workplace effectiveness

BACKGROUND AND THEORY

The Xerox Corporation in the USA was one of three corporations that took part in a now-classic experiment in the early 1990s to find ways of changing working practices to enhance gender equity, including work–personal life integration. This was part of a programme sponsored by the Ford Foundation, involving collaboration between a Xerox team and a team of action researchers led by Rhona Rapoport and Lotte Bailyn.[1] The action research team looked at working practices through what they initially called a work–family lens[2] (and later a gender-equity lens), to identify general work and cultural assumptions that made it difficult for all employees—not just those with current family commitments—to integrate their work and personal lives. Then they collaborated in the design of experiments to achieve changes in working

---

[1] The team also included Susan Eaton, Joyce Fletcher, Maureen Harvey, Robin Johnson, Deborah Kolb and Lesley Perlow.

[2] Although their initial concern was gender equity the team found it more acceptable initially to talk about work–family. Later, they were able to refer to a gender-equity rather than work–family lens. See Rapoport et al. (2002) for a fuller account of the Xerox case and other cases using this approach.

practices to address these barriers. What they found was that innovations to address these issues enhanced not only employees' opportunities for harmonising work and personal life, but also productivity. The outcomes were win–win solutions addressing a dual agenda for change. It gradually became apparent that only by rethinking workplace practices, to meet the dual agenda of workplace effectiveness and employee work–personal life integration, could sustainable and fundamental change be achieved.

This approach is informed by a recognition that the assumptions on which most workplace practices are based are embedded in a cultural myth of separate and gendered spheres of work and employment, on the one hand, regarded as primarily the domain of men, and family and personal life, on the other hand, regarded as primarily the domain of women. The ideology of separate spheres fails to recognise that most people have commitments in both domains. It sustains the view that the ideal worker is one who does not have any other responsibilities and commitments beyond employment. So, many working practices fail to take account of workers' needs for time and energy for personal life beyond work (Bailyn & Fletcher, 2003; Fletcher & Rapoport, 1996; Rapoport et al., 2002).

The myth of separate and gendered spheres also leads to the valuing of different types of behaviour. There is an assumption that stereotypically masculine characteristics are necessary to be effective in the workplace and stereotypically feminine characteristics are necessary in the family sphere. Thus, traditionally masculine values and behaviours, such as "firefighting" and competitiveness, come to be associated with the ideal worker while more traditionally feminine characteristics, such as interpersonal skills and collaboration, are undervalued in workplace settings. Conflating idealised masculinity with the ideal worker obviously creates difficulties for women in the workplace, but also makes it difficult for men to integrate their work and personal lives. It defines commitment in terms of willingness to work long hours and lack of involvement in family life or other domains, and defines competence and what is considered to be "real work" in ways that perpetuate inefficient ways of working. The action research approach illustrated in this case study at the Xerox Corporation challenges these assumptions and demonstrates that they undermine workplace effectiveness as well as quality of life.

THE COMPANY

At this time Xerox was perceived as a very progressive company because it had implemented many family-friendly policies. Nevertheless, there continued to be problems retaining and promoting women. It was recognised that work–family policies alone were not sufficient to move towards a more equitable workplace.

The action researchers worked collaboratively with a Xerox planning group at three very different sites: a product development team, a customer administration centre and a sales, service and business operations partnership, each located in different areas of the United States. There were comprehensive work–family policies and a willingness to respond to work–family needs, but this was having limited impact: men were reluctant to take up these possibilities and those women who did so felt that they sacrificed career advancement. Thus individual accommodation for specific employees—usually women—failed to achieve systemic change in basic structures, cultures and working practices. The organisation was *accommodating* to the needs of its diverse workforce, but not learning or fundamentally changing working practices and the assumptions on which they were based. The ideal employee remained one who worked full time and as though they had no family responsibilities; a situation that remains very common in a wide range of organisations and locations (Lewis, 1997; Lewis, Cooper et al., 2003; Lewis, Rapoport et al., 2003). Indeed, the Xerox research team concluded that this individual, work–family-policy-based approach not only failed to achieve wide change but actually inhibited more systemic innovation because it was believed that the company had "dealt with" work–family issues (Fletcher & Rapoport, 1996).

TRADITIONAL ASSUMPTIONS CHALLENGED IN THIS CASE STUDY

● Family and other non-work issues are individual concerns that are not relevant to work performance and have nothing to do with business success.

- People who make time for family or other personal commitments cannot be good employees.

- Working long hours is the most effective way of getting work done.

- Only workers prepared to put in long hours are effective and therefore valuable.

- Managers must always retain discretion about employee flexibility— employees cannot be trusted to keep in mind the interests of the organisation as well as their own interests.

- It is necessary to have formal procedures to restrict and contain flexibility—it will not work if everyone can use it.

- Working with continual deadline crises is often inevitable and so firefighting (macho) skills are more valuable than planning or crisis prevention skills.

- It is OK for people to be interrupted by supervisors during the working day because they can always make up the time after normal working hours.

- You have to be aggressive to get on in business. Individualism and competitiveness are more useful approaches than collaboration.

- It is important to maintain boundaries between specialisms.

INTRODUCING CHANGE

This section describes the methods used and illustrates how changes were achieved in each of the three sites. The process was the same at each site, but innovations and outcomes were unique to each context.

Collaborative Interactive Action Research

Collaborative interactive action research (CIAR), the method used in the Xerox case, is a specific form of action research. Within an organisational context action research can be understood as research that stems from an involvement by a researcher or research team with members of an organisation that relates to problems or concerns, where there is an intention by organisational members to take action based on the research and intervention (Eden & Huxham, 1999). It usually involves the building of theories about the reasons for particular organisational problems and experimentation with interventions developed on the basis of this theory (Argyris & Schon, 1991).

The change process in the Xerox case was developed using a form of action research that the researchers came to call collaborative interactive action research (CIAR). This emphasizes the importance of collaboration, joint exploration and mutual learning, with a focus on understanding interactions within workplaces. Informed by insights about the impact of gendered separate spheres' ideology and the dual agenda, the research element refers to a process of surfacing underlying assumptions in organisations and the ways in which these lead to working practices that can undermine equity and work–personal life integration at the same time as they impede effectiveness. The action element of CIAR is the commitment not only to learn but also to take action to try to bring about change, from how things are now to how they could be.

The action research programme began with a concern about gender equity, although the researchers found it more acceptable to talk about work and family within organisations initially. It was recognised that work–family policies were not bringing about fundamental change and that it was necessary to reframe the issues to get beyond the individual approach of helping particular employees to manage their unique work and family problems towards a more systemic reconsideration of organisational norms, values and structures that underpinned inequitable workplaces and also undermined performance. So, the focus moved from work–family policies to working practices that were making it difficult for people to integrate their work and personal life and also undermining workplace effectiveness.

CIAR as a process of mutual enquiry involving researchers and work teams yields new ways of thinking about issues within organisations. It is based on a model of research in which data-gathering, feedback and interventions take place concurrently at individual and group levels throughout the process. The aim of the researchers is that, once they have completed their work, they will leave behind a stance of ongoing enquiry (rather than just specific changes), that connects work to family and other personal life domains, links work–personal life issues to the way that work is accomplished and does so in a way that is equitable for men and women (Fletcher & Rapoport, 1996).

CIAR involves the following steps:

- *Starting with a salient business need.*

- *Looking at working practices with work units through a work–family/ work–personal life/gender-equity lens including legitimising taboo issues.*

- *Keeping the dual agenda in focus at all times—dropping either the effectiveness or the work–personal life integration goal—prevents positive outcomes.*

- *Working collaboratively to develop mutual understandings of working practices, underlying assumptions and their impact on the dual agenda.*

- *Working collaboratively to think of innovative solutions.*

- *Experimenting with new ways of working.*

- *Engaging with resistance as a positive force throughout.*

- *Evaluating interventions and communicating outcomes to diffuse organisational learning.*

Starting with a Salient Business Need

The process began with the identification of salient business needs (usually these are identified by senior management, although other issues can arise, especially in interviews with employees, and are taken into account within the process). At Xerox there were different issues at each site.

At the Customer Administration Centre where the workforce comprised largely women, many with family commitments, there were high levels of unexpected absence, resulting in problems of lack of cover. There was also high staff turnover. Management were attempting to shift the structure towards more empowered self-managed teams so that staff could manage their own absences ensuring cover at all time, but this was not proceeding smoothly.

The largely male product development team was highly stressed, working under constant pressure to get products to market in the shortest possible time, but not succeeding in doing so despite working long hours.

At the sales, service and business operations partnership there was also a high level of pressure, especially relating to increasing targets in sales and the need for constant availability in service. There were very poor relationships between sales and service, with poor communications and a lack of collaboration which caused problems for customers.

Looking at Working Practices through a Work–Family/Work–Personal Life/ Gender-Equity and also Efficiency Lens. Working Collaboratively to Develop Mutual Understandings of Working Practices, Underlying Assumptions and Their Impact on the Dual Agenda.
Working Collaboratively to Design Solutions.
Experimenting with New Ways of Working

The CIAR approach aimed to uncover work patterns grounded in unquestioned assumptions, rules, values and norms, which reinforced working practices that made it difficult for employees to integrate their employment and personal lives, and also undermined business effectiveness. That is, work–personal life integration issues were used as a catalyst for systemic organisational change drawing on the synergy of the dual agenda. Working practices were examined in terms of their impact on both work–personal life integration for employees and workplace effectiveness to draw out possible implications for changing practices, structures and cultures.

This involved the research team working with work units—groups of people who worked together—to focus on the ways in which work was carried out. The idea was to identify working practices based on gendered assumptions and to make visible their costs and consequences in terms of the dual agenda of effectiveness and work–personal life integration. Customary working practices tend to appear natural, normal and gender-neutral, so it is necessary to identify, surface and challenge those assumptions that are sustaining inequity and ineffectiveness. Identifying these work practices provides leverage points for change.

The research into working practices and underlying assumptions involved a range of methods of data collection, including surveys, observation, shadowing individual employees, attending technical and staff meetings and collaborative individual interviews, with managers, supervisors and line workers. Individual interviews provided a context in which topics that were taboo in the workplace, about personal needs, could be explored. All types of workers in the target groups participated in the collaborative interviews, regardless of whether or not they had family commitments. These interviews aimed to engage people in micro-interventions by pushing them to think about the reasons for their taken-for-granted working practices. They were asked to respond to questions such as: What is recognised as competence here? What is viewed as real work? How is time used? How is commitment assessed? Does this affect men and women differently? How? But, there were also discussions about their personal lives, aiming to break the taboo about discussing personal issues in relation to work and making the consideration of personal issues equally as important as work issues.

The action research group then analysed the findings in terms of the dual agenda, and discussed their initial interpretations and themes with a work unit at each site. The research team and work units collaborated in trying to understand the themes emerging from the analysis in terms of assumptions underlying work practices that were inequitable and ineffective and considering the consequences of these assumptions for the dual agenda, so that they could come to a shared understanding of what factors were holding back performance and work–personal life integration. Employing the notion of fluid expertise, as discussed in Chapter 1, the researchers did not impose their perspectives, but transferred expertise between the work group and the research group as appropriate so that mutual learning could take place. This helped to reframe the issues which could then be related to specific business needs, which differed on each site.

The next stage was to seek solutions to dual agenda issues. This addressed the question: How can we help people to be able to integrate their work and personal lives and also improve our effectiveness? Collaborative problem-solving that legitimised discussions of employees' personal needs as well as business goals helped to engage people's creativity and enable them to work towards sustainable solutions. Once innovations were introduced people were committed to making them work because of the personal as well as business pay-offs.

Innovations were then piloted in the context of a moratorium—a period of time in which no judgements were made. Change takes time and employees had to feel safe and know that they would not be judged by initial performance.

When making change it was essential to keep the dual agenda on the table. If either side of the equation is dropped interventions are not successful.

We now turn to exploring some assumptions that emerged overall, especially relating to time, and the specific processes at each Xerox site.

ASSUMPTIONS ABOUT TIME IN THE THREE PROJECTS

This process of surfacing assumptions helped to identify assumptions about time which were based on gendered notions of the ideal worker and the separate spheres' ideology (ideal workers do not have substantial family involvement and the undervaluing of competencies more stereotypically associated with women). These emerged as very important in each site, although they were played out in different ways.

In sales and in engineering there was an assumption that long hours were necessary to get work done. Those with family commitments—most likely to be women—were less likely to be able to put in long hours and therefore less valued. In administration there were assumptions about flexibility and time—employees were not trusted to manage their own time flexibility and sustain productivity. In service there was an issue of uncertainty about time—not knowing when employees would be called upon to work unexpectedly—thought to be an essential aspect of the job. All these assumptions about time were viewed as inevitable and the working practices that resulted viewed as necessary to be productive. The research team questioned the beliefs about time in each site because of the obvious link with work–personal life integration. In each case they found that these assumptions were also counterproductive in terms of business needs. By making these connections with specific business needs at each site and working collaboratively with work teams it was possible to identify interventions to address the dual agenda, uniquely for each context.

Interventions to change working practices and assumptions were then developed collaboratively. Work redesign needs the experience of those who do the job and really know the situation. Outside researchers cannot provide answers—solutions must be developed collaboratively and interactively. The interactive nature of the process is key throughout the process. The process also helps team members to overcome taboos by bringing personal needs into the picture, so that these, as well as business needs, can be taken into account in problem-solving. A range of solutions were designed by employees working with action researchers, addressing the specific issues emerging in each context.

Customer Administration

In customer administration it emerged that a culture of control by management was undermining the goal of empowerment. Although there was a range of work–personal life policies available management were reluctant to allow employees to use them as they feared that this would undermine productivity. Consequently, employees, who were mainly women at this site, had to make their own arrangements to try to juggle work and family commitments. Often, these arrangements broke down, so they would have to call in sick or use vacation time. This led to high levels of unexpected absence, with such problems as lack of cover, backlash against those who did take up work–family policies, high staff turnover and general mistrust of the organisation.

Surfacing these assumptions—systemic rather than individual—enabled managers to reflect on their reluctance to give up control because of short-term productivity concerns and they came to understand why they were experiencing so much difficulty moving towards empowered teams. They realised the negative consequences of the culture of control. In response to this the team designed an experiment in which work–family policies were made available to all, regardless of family situation or management discretion. Ultimately, there was a move away from individual accommodation to meet the needs of specific employees, and from elaboration (see Chapter 1), where flexibility is contained through control and procedures, to tranformative learning and systemic change where flexibility became ingrained in the culture. The outcome was that teams came up with collective approaches to flexibility to meet productivity and personal needs.

This resulted in a 30% decrease in absenteeism. In addition, customer responsiveness increased as times of coverage were extended. Employee satisfaction also improved. It became possible to move to more self-managed teams who gradually took on more responsibility and participated in decisions about work schedules. It would not have been possible to move straight to this level of flexibility without going through this process and involving and collaborating with all the team.

Product Development

In the product development team of professional engineers, work–personal life issues were not explicitly discussed, but long working hours, perceived as essential, made life difficult for most workers. They tended to work continually in crisis mode, with long and usually unpredictable hours, trying to meet the business goal of shortening time to market. Using a work–family lens (i.e., acknowledging the difficulties experienced) also helped to understand the problems in meeting this business goal. It became clear that the reason for this continual crisis mode was a work culture that rewarded long hours at work and individual problem-solving. People were rewarded more for solving crises that they had created themselves than for preventing crises. Management recognised that the problems caused by continual crises and long hours were interfering with the team's ability to get products to market in a timely fashion, but had not managed to change this because they had not confronted the underlying cultural assumptions about work. They also failed to recognise their own role in interrupting engineers too often, thereby extending the length of the working day.

The research team challenged the way time was allocated and helped work groups take control over their use of time. For example, one group restructured their work day to include periods of quiet, uninterrupted time and time for interactions. Freed from the assumptions that they must work long hours to be good at their jobs, they began to look for ways in which they could better structure their time to prevent crises and work more efficiently.

The collaboratively designed interventions challenged prevailing norms by identifying skills of problem prevention and working towards developing systems for rewarding these, rather than the more macho firefighting skills. The way work was allocated was also questioned. This led to a clearer differentiation between essential and unnecessary interruptions and enabled more planning and crises prevention, rather than just crisis management.

The interventions in the product management teams had the effect of reducing time to market. The team achieved its first on-time launch of a new product, and a number of excellence awards.

The District Partnership

At the district partnership of sales, service and business operations, assumptions were identified which undermined effective collaboration between different departments. In a highly competitive environment, individualism was the norm with very limited collaboration between sales, service and business operations, although in theory they were supposed to work in "partnership". The CIAR process helped them to question assumptions about the specialisation and functional separation that was resulting in a failure to share information about customers. Moreover, they rarely helped each other out if there were family issues or emergencies. This created problems for sales, service and customer responsiveness as well as for work–personal life integration. As Lotte Bailyn and her colleagues explain:

> ... *appealing to employees' work–family concerns can provide the motivation and energy for productive efforts at reengineering and restructuring.*
>
> Rapoport, Bailyn, Fletcher & Pruitt (2002, p. 17)

This is what happened here. The work team and the action researchers collaborated to restructure the ways that the different functions worked together in order to both help work–family integration and enhance customer service. They found new and surprising ways of working together. For example, the service team helped sales to identify new markets and sales helped service to plan their operations better. Through better communications and a more collective collaborative approach the different functions found ways of working together, even covering for each other, and became more responsive to customers.

Ultimately, members of the team were able to count on each other for coverage, including across functions, and to plan and predict family time better. Sales increased and service and customer responsiveness improved, despite downsizing and growing external competition at this time.

ENGAGE WITH RESISTANCE THROUGHOUT

Some resistance to challenges to current working practices is inevitable, especially as these practices are likely to have appeared successful in the past. However, resistance is regarded as an integral part of the process, providing important insights in the assumptions underpinning normative work practices. In CIAR, resistance is regarded as positive and crucial for learning to take progress. There is always resistance and it is very important to work with it and not sweep it under the carpet. In fact, it has been argued that CIAR researchers should question whether they are on the right track if there is no resistance (Rapoport et al., 2002).

Because of the power of the separate spheres' ideology the research team at Xerox experienced considerable resistance to the connection between work–personal life issues and business goals. They were continually asked what work–family (as it was expressed at this stage) had to do with work (Fletcher and Rapoport, 1996).

Working with resistance involves uncovering concerns, such as how work will get done if people do not stay late to do it or whether part-time workers can be as engaged as full timers. Working with individuals to explore their concerns in terms of the dual agenda and emphasizing both aspects of this dual agenda is important.

This approach takes time and requires people to reflect on why they work in the way that they do, considering systemic and not only individual explanations. It does not offer quick fixes, but has the potential to achieve fundamental and sustainable change. Another form of resistance is reluctance to spend the time needed to achieve this level of insight, collaboration and change (see Chapter 4), despite the potential benefits. As Rhona Rapoport explains:

> The whole process takes time. It is important to take time to reflect and understand at the beginning of the process. For many people it is counter intuitive to think that taking time for the process will have long term benefits, but it is essential.

As pilot interventions progress and "small wins" are achieved it becomes easier to challenge resistance.

DIFFUSION

While transformational learning took place in these three parts of the organisation, wider organisational learning requires that the process is diffused more widely. The research team at Xerox were aware that they did not get to diffuse the findings well beyond the three participating departments and regard this as an important task for the future. There are many questions about how this can be achieved. For example, must there be an outsider working with the company all the time? Can an insider take over to carry forward and diffuse the process? Would insider/outsider partnerships be more effective? These questions are addressed in subsequent chapters.

SUMMARY OF SOME OF THE OUTCOMES

- 30% decrease in absenteeism at one site.

- Customer responsiveness increased as times of coverage were extended.

- Employee satisfaction improved.

- The goal of moving to more self-managed teams, which had previously been resisted, was achieved and they gradually took on more responsibility and participated in decisions about work schedules.

- Restructuring of time and working practices reduced the need to work in constant crisis mode and resulted in success in shortening time to get products to market.

- Enhanced collaboration and working across specialisation resulted in increase in sales and improved service and customer responsiveness improved, despite downsizing and growing external competition.

LEEDS METROPOLITAN UNIVERSITY LIBRARY

LESSONS LEARNED FROM THIS CASE STUDY

- Working practices that undermine gender-equity and work–personal life integration also undermine work effectiveness.

- These practices tend to be based on gendered assumptions about the nature of commitment and valuing of certain competencies more than others.

- Collaboration with people external to the organisation who do not take for granted that everyday working practices and routines can be helpful in surfacing counterproductive assumptions on which they are based.

- Collaborative interactive action research (which involves looking at working practices through a work–family/work–life/gender-equity and effectiveness lens, keeping the dual agenda in focus, listening, reflecting and experimenting) is a useful process for developing win–win innovations.

- The surfacing of gendered assumptions and identification of how these impact on the dual agenda, and the linking of these to specific business needs helps to reframe the issues and look for innovative solutions.

- Assumptions about time and competence are important barriers to fundamental change, but these are played out in different ways in diverse contexts.

- Effective solutions are designed collaboratively, drawing on the expertise of those carrying out the work as well as insights of action researchers.

- Interventions to change working practices work best when they are collaboratively developed to meet the goals of a dual agenda of work–personal life integration and workplace effectiveness (i.e., win–win solutions).

- There is no single good practice. Different innovations will be optimal in different workplaces in relation to specific business needs and issues.

- Legitimising discussions of employees' personal needs as well as business goals helps to engage people's creativity in order to reach sustainable solutions.

- Resistance is inevitable and useful. It is important to surface and work with resistance.

- Solutions developed through this process do not have negative costs for the organisation and can have very substantial bottom-line benefits.

CHAPTER 3

Energyco[1]

Building on bottom-up initiatives for flexible working in a large corporation

TRANSFORMATION—BUT NOT YET ORGANISATION-WIDE

The researchers in the Xerox case recognised that they did not have the opportunity to diffuse the learning from the pilot experiments across the entire organisation and that this would be an important task for the future. The case of Energyco discussed in this chapter demonstrates how bottom-up initiatives can be used creatively to bring about systemic change in parts of the organisation with some wider diffusion of learning. However, it also highlights the pitfalls of incomplete diffusion of learning across the organisation, when changing expectations of flexibility of work are not shared by all managers.

Energyco is a large international industrial corporation headquartered in one of the Nordic countries and competing in a global context. Like most industries in today's economy the workforce includes a large proportion of knowledge workers. At the beginning of the case study senior management recognised that a pool of talented employees and

[1] Pseudonym. All remaining case studies use a pseudonym.

flexibility to respond to or anticipate changing conditions would be vital for the company's future survival in the global market. Workplace flexibility was in keeping with the home country's laws and welfare policies, such as progressive parental leave policies, which can contribute, over time, to a new set of norms. There was a strong belief in the connection between availability of flexible forms of working and ability of the organisation to attract and retain the most talented and competent employees, and this provided the rationale for the change process discussed in this chapter. There was already a culture of substantial empowerment and minimal central control in most parts of the business, which facilitated the emergence of innovative forms of working, upon which the change process built.

This existing culture of empowerment provided a context in which various flexible forms of working had been developed spontaneously and collaboratively by knowledge workers in some sections of the business. In particular, these included initiatives to enable employees to work at home or at other locations, to save on commuting time (benefiting employees and the company) and increase flexibility to integrate their work with other activities as well as enabling the company to relocate people more easily. These initiatives included:

- Home offices comprising an office at employees' homes with computer, ISDN phone and data line and a router.

- Mobile offices involving the provision of a laptop and mobile phone for the options of working at different locations and keeping in touch with colleagues (e.g., while travelling and commuting, on trains and buses or at airports or hotels). Since the company has employees in several locations nationally, many are transferred to another office without moving their families. Hence, mobile offices enabled them to use valuable commuting time on a weekly or daily basis.

- Mobile solutions involving the same equipment plus ISDN line and router at home. Other initiatives (not discussed here) included changing office layouts at the workplace to enhance flexibility and communication while in the office, as well as saving on office space.

The objectives of these initiatives was flexibility of working time and place which would also contribute to flexibility of the organisation to adapt to changing conditions. Ultimately, the success of such initiatives depends on acceptance of the different ways of working facilitated by these solutions as valuable for the organisation and not just individuals. This was successful in many (but not all) parts of the company.

The traditional *assumptions challenged* by this process, where it was successful, are that:

- Employees need to be visible at the workplace to work effectively and demonstrate commitment.

- Employees are not trustworthy or self-motivated.

- Employees need a fixed location to work, in a central office.

- Flexibility of working time and place is constrained by laws, regulations and union agreements.

INTRODUCING CHANGE

Senior management recognised the potential value of the emerging innovations to the organisation, so an attempt was made to systematically evaluate these bottom-up initiatives and to examine whether and how they might be appropriate and valuable to implement more widely. Four bottom-up initiatives were designed as pilot experiments in an attempt to evaluate the potential of local initiatives in terms of wider strategies and organisational learning. In these parallel pilot experiments a team of researchers were brought in and pulled together a number of innovations initiated by work teams in order to see how they worked in or could be adapted to diverse contexts and to assess their impact on different stakeholders (i.e., the organisation, the workplace, the individual employee and the family).

The researchers used elements of an action research model, collaborating in discussions and the change process. Different initiatives were piloted in four separate units, including an IT support unit in which 80 out of 600 employees participated, a resource and consultancy unit in which 50 out of 800 employees participated, and two further units dealing with technology and with communications. The pilot projects were limited in scope and time, each with a clearly defined content. However, learning is a long-term process and continues beyond the period of the pilot experiments. All pilot projects worked towards the same strategic goals (i.e., win–win flexible working solutions benefiting both the employer and the employees).

Pilot projects were selected for the experiments through collaboration between senior management and work units. Project management set visions and strategy for the project as a whole—but individual pilot groups set explicit goals and strategies for their own pilot experiments within this. Corporate sponsorship from the top is important because it provides a feeling of safety and a moratorium from past and current policies and practices within which to experiment.

A corporate steering group was established to support the researchers and to oversee and pull together the results of the pilot projects, but the day-to-day running was left to the piloting units which had considerable autonomy. In addition, a core team of each of the four pilot co-ordinators discussed emerging themes and were members of and reported to the steering group. The actual experiments however, remained bottom-up (i.e., employees collaborated and brainstormed, together with the action researchers who facilitated the process, about adjustments over time and the best ways of doing things).

In addition, union representatives were involved in all stages to ensure that they were included in the decision processes. One important output from the pilots was the realisation that much more flexibility was possible within current laws and regulations than most had anticipated. (There are strict regulations about working time and relatively strong trade unions in the Nordic countries.) Another important output was a set of guidelines which included guidance on how to ensure that flexible working arrangements can be achieved within current laws and regulations, including working time and tax laws.

The pilot experiments were evaluated by the collection of mainly qualitative data: document analysis, observation, interviews and surveys.

LEARNING POINTS FROM THE PILOT EXPERIMENTS

The Need for Flexible Flexibility

The pilot units were different groups with diverse contexts and needs, so there was no notion of streamlining one example as *the best* practice. Win–win solutions must be adapted to meet the needs of each specific context. As a vice-president put it:

> Flexible arrangements should be flexible. It is not a change to a new rigid system. What works in one context might not work in another.

The Dual Agenda

Change processes leading to win–win solutions locally depend on creativity and "tailoring" to specific needs. Therefore, it was recognised as important not to have too much structure and guidelines at the outset. At the same time there was also a recognition that for flexibility to be really effective, it must meet the needs of all stakeholders:

> If we are going to obtain win–win solutions through flexible work it must be suitable and conducive to the unit and the work require-ments. It should not cause extra work for colleagues and it should be satisfactory/suitable ... for the employee and his/her family.

Focus on Output Rather than Input

In evaluating the pilots it was necessary to get beyond time- or input-based criteria and move to output criteria. That is, the focus was on work produced and not on the place where work is carried out and the time taken to produce it. This is not always straightforward, of course, and output criteria are easier to formulate in some types of work than others (Felstead, Jewson & Walters, 2003).

Example of Working Flexibly

Erik's job at Energyco involved much international travel. He had important contacts and skills that were crucial for the business. His wife was an architect but had slowed down her career while they had young children. Her employer had been very flexible because Erik travelled so much. Then Erik and his wife decided it was her turn to focus on her career and that Energyco should be more flexible and allow Erik to work differently. His manager agreed that he could work reduced hours (just a little less than full time) and work from home or from mobile locations. He was able to keep up with his worldwide contacts by email and mobile phone. As clients were often in different time zones he was actually able to communicate with them better than if he had been always in the office and in addition was able to cut down on travel expenses, visiting overseas only when it was essential.

His productivity remained at least as high as it had been previously and international clients were impressed by the flexibility and innovation of the company.

BOTTOM-UP APPROACHES WITH TOP-DOWN SUPPORT

One of the learning points was that *although it is good to have the units developing innovative ideas themselves, support from the top was also essential*. Some felt that corporate involvement could have been even greater. Even though the steering group comprised middle- to high-level management, they argued that if the CEO and the top management are not fully supportive, this can result in a gap between espoused values and actual practice—and lack of such support may hold back sustainable solutions. There was a recognition that if the level of engagement of senior management is not sufficiently high this can lead to an implementation gap or to a "retreat" to old practices.

LEARNING BY DOING, REFLECTING AND DISCUSSING

The parallel pilots stimulated constructive discussions between the pilot groups as well as within them, reinforcing "learning by doing", which is crucial for organisational learning.

If participants' personal experiences with the changes were positive, this led to "small wins" (see Rapoport, Bailyn, Fletcher & Pruitt, 2002); that is, the achievement of small goals, which further reinforced positive attitudes towards change. During the pilot projects, employees, in collaboration with the action researchers, often adopted new solutions and moved on to focus on other issues and make new changes. So, this provided the impetus for exploring and innovating—testing new ideas.

DEVELOPING A NEW LANGUAGE OF FLEXIBILITY

Throughout the pilot experiments new concepts and new under-standings of existing language developed and this helped to articulate learning and developments. For example, the term *flexible work forms* was already used, but this was originally assumed to apply only to home office and portable solutions. During the experiments this was expanded to include central-office-based solutions, such as "hot-desking" or easy-to-change office spaces. There was a view that managers need to develop arenas for discussion to encourage and facilitate collaborative under-standings and diffusion of new ideas.

An example of an innovation facilitated by the new concepts and language of flexible working and the subsequent creative thinking is the 24-hour operations implemented by the Information Services division, subsequent to the original experiments. In order that all Energyco employees around the world can get the best possible service if, for example, their PC is not working properly, a worldwide support team has been built up to provide the assistance at any time. The service consists of three hubs: one in the home country, one in the USA and the third in the Far East. Energyco employees can call and talk to people who will answer computer queries and solve PC problems at any time. The idea is for the hubs to be staffed at the times when people in the same or adjacent time zones are at work. This "follow-the-sun" concept ensures that the caller will always be able to talk to an alert and wide-awake troubleshooter.

ENGAGING WITH RESISTANCE

The notion of resistance as a positive force to work towards change was not explicitly present. Nevertheless, resistance was noted from various groups and it was recognised that this had to be worked with and negotiated. For example, one of the women employees was on maternity leave and wanted to work part time and be able to follow the developments at work from her home office. Her manager agreed, but the "employee association" said that the law required that she take full maternity leave, even though she had requested this arrangement. Finally, a deal was negotiated whereby she could do some work at home during the period of her maternity leave, which suited all concerned. Resistance from other sources in the wider organisation were not surfaced and caused some difficulties as discussed later in this case study. In particular, many managers experience great difficulties in managing remote, non-visible workers (Felstead et al., 2003) and there are complex issues and assumptions here that need to be worked through collaboratively.

IMPORTANCE OF WIDER CONTEXT

The home country's laws and welfare policies support flexible working. Similarly, the strict regulations about working time and relatively strong trade unions have not, as many might fear, undermined opportunities for flexibility, due to the collaborative process within which they have been developed. The practices developed at Energyco's headquarters are gradually influencing working practices at locations where national policies are less developed.

DIFFUSION AND ORGANISATIONAL LEARNING

A major challenge is how to diffuse the learning from the pilot experiments more widely. Does everyone have to learn by doing, going through the process, or can ideas be diffused by those who have undergone experiential learning? An attempt to encourage learning beyond the pilot of groups was made by keeping the projects open and visible and encouraging continuous information-sharing. Benefits of this included the following:

- Making the pilot participants visible to others created a commitment to the process and a sense of pride among participants. It also strengthened accountability.

- It invited discussions about what happened in the project. These are important for reflection and learning.

People who had been involved in the changes were useful ambassadors when diffusing the process and its benefits to the wider organisation and this helped to avoid a "not invented here" or "it wouldn't work here" effect.

Interactions and discussions during and after the pilot period enabled the development of a common understanding and organisational learning within much of the organisation. It achieved change at an accelerated pace in a win–win direction. Nevertheless, pockets of resistance remained and were not all worked with, so diffusion across the company was uneven.

UNEVEN LEARNING AND SUPPORT FOR FLEXIBLE WORKING TIME AND PLACE

The pilot projects contributed to systemic structural and cultural changes in parts of the organisation. But, not all units were willing to learn from the experiments—especially if they had not been through the process themselves. Some lagged behind and would not join in the bottom-up process of thinking about different, non-traditional ways of working and there was an understandable reluctance among senior management to push resistant sections to experiment. A vice-president said:

> ... we have a culture and tradition that things like this should be bottom up. We shouldn't force things like this on a particular unit, because if they are unwilling they probably wouldn't do a good job. They may be afraid that it may turn out really badly.

Deep change means moving people beyond their comfort zones and can be difficult. The pilot experiments helped to overcome resistance to change in some parts of the organisation, especially through being able to demonstrate small wins. But, after the pilots some resistance remained and proved difficult to engage with, particularly in older, more traditional divisions with more of a hierarchical structure than other newer sections. So, when, for example, Olav, encouraged by the new talk of valuing flexible working arrangements, went to his boss to ask if he could work 80% of full time, including working at home, he was told that he was regarded as not being serious about his job and career. In this part of the business there remained an assumption that commitment had to be demonstrated by face time in the workplace. His manager was persuaded, reluctantly, to allow him to work in this way for a short time. He was able to be very productive, working flexibly. But, shortly afterwards his job was cut. He was offered another job that was not very attractive, and so was indirectly forced to resign. He is now working as an independent consultant. So, the company lost a highly committed worker with enormous skills, knowledge and contacts, not easily replaced. Energyco lost his expertise and many of his international clients because of the reluctance of this unit to genuinely experiment with flexible forms of working.

Now, management in this division are beginning to realise that they will be obliged to be open to a wider range of ways of working if they are to recruit and retain the best staff. But, it was a difficult lesson for them to learn. In part, the problem stemmed from traditional management, mostly senior men with non-career wives, and may change as management personnel changes. However, this example demonstrates that it is difficult to change the assumptions that sustain traditional working methods without learning by collaboration and by experience. Diffusion of learning is not always easy.

SOME OUTCOMES

Benefits to the Corporation

- The pilot-testing of many different innovations in parallel helped to illustrate *the need for flexible solutions to be embedded in specific contexts* to meet diverse operational and employee needs. Most participants believed after piloting that the project did contribute towards the organisation's ability to change and to adapt to changing circumstances over time and place.

- There were clear savings to the organisation with regard to office space and also increased effectiveness in terms of employees being better able to work when it was convenient both for the company and themselves, or when they felt "inspired" rather than distracted. However, it was found that this requires self-discipline on the part of the individual to avoid the tendency to work too much. This is a problem that has been widely noted in research (Felstead et al., 2003; Prutchno, Litchfield & Fried, 2000; Sullivan & Lewis, 2001).

- As a result of these pilots, flexible work forms have been implemented in numerous units throughout the business, each adapted to the particular and local needs of the specific context. Employees and their managers are encouraged to question traditional assumptions about effective work practices and to think creatively about flexible ways of working. As one employee working flexibly put it:

> *Flexibility is like a tool that optimises productivity and makes it possible to have a private life along with a demanding job. Smart companies recognize that people are more conscious about quality-of-life issues these days, and respond. If they don't make flexibility a strategy, they won't get a diversity of employees.*

However, setting up expectations of support for flexibility of time and place also had adverse consequences when not all managers were on board.

NO CAUSE FOR COMPLACENCY. THE NEED TO SUSTAIN THE PROCESS

Some years after the original experiments there are now new people in senior management positions in the organisation who had not been through the processes or learned from experience. A major challenge is to ensure that new people are on board and to help them to understand the process whereby bottom-up solutions with top-down support can help to meet the needs of multiple stakeholders. In some units there is still reluctance to look at working practices and ways in which they could be changed to suit individual needs. Nevertheless, the flexibility experiments have encouraged many units to develop adaptable forms of organization, offices and work, with very positive consequences—and while central or corporate oversight would support a change to new work practices, the lack of this central control also allows those units that want new solutions to implement these within the guidelines.

This case study illustrates the uneven nature of learning in a large organisation. There have thus been pockets of transformational organisational learning within Energyco. However, as in many large organisations going through this process there are also pockets of resistance which have yet to be confronted, where learning has not progressed beyond the elaboration stage. Assumptions about the need for employee visibility remains strong in some parts of the organisation and in these contexts there remains a concern to limit and contain flexibility.

LESSONS LEARNED FROM THIS CASE STUDY

- A culture of empowerment can create the conditions for the spontaneous emergence of innovative ways of working flexibly.

- Parallel pilot experiments with specific goals and time frames, including collaboration with action researchers, can help to explore the wider implications, applicability and benefits of such innovations.

- Collaboration at all levels is key: a combination of bottom-up initiatives and top-down support and strategic vision, with the inclusion of union representatives in decision making, builds widespread ownership of change.

- Top-level sponsorship is essential for minimising feelings of risk.

- Strong unions and strict regulation of working time need not limit opportunities for flexibility, providing that there is good collaboration and understanding of how to operate creatively within the regulations.

- The change process depends on creativity and this is facilitated by having very minimal guidelines and structures.

- Flexibility works best when it addresses a dual or multiple agenda, meeting the needs of multiple stakeholders.

- Care must be taken that flexible solutions do not just become new rigidities, but remain truly flexible. People can easily retreat to new comfort zones.

- The most effective learning about flexibility comes through experience of "doing" flexibility.

- Evaluation of flexible working must be in terms of output and not input (time at work).

- Opportunities to reflect on and discuss new flexible forms of work, through social interaction within groups and across the organisation, help to create new language to support flexibility.

- Diffusion of new ideas is very effective when it is undertaken by internal people who have first-hand experience of flexible working within the organisation.

- Some managers feared that non-visible employees may not work hard enough, but there is also a danger that when employees have complete flexibility they may work too hard.

- Some resistance is inevitable, and usually useful. Often, this can be engaged with and solutions found through collaboration and negotiation.

- When resistance is not engaged with, this can undermine the broader diffusion of transformational organisational learning. The effects of raising expectations about culture change when it is not widely diffused can be damaging to individual careers and organisational effectiveness.

- Outcomes include:
  - ○ Savings in office space.
  - ○ Increased effectiveness as employees work when it is convenient both for the company and themselves, or when they feel "inspired" rather than distracted.
  - ○ Enhanced recruitment and retention of talented and experienced employees.
  - ○ Resentment and frustration when flexibility is not consistently applied.

Change is an ongoing process and momentum has to be encouraged or sustained especially among those who have not learned by experience—such as new senior management and more traditional departments.

CHAPTER 4

Proffirm—The Professional Practice Firm

The significance of time

BACKGROUND

Proffirm is a consultancy practice, part of a large international organisation providing professional advice and services on an hourly fees basis. Although there was no shortage of new recruits to the firm there was high turnover, especially among younger staff. A range of work–life policies had been developed by the HR department to try to enhance retention, but take-up of these initiatives was low. It was mainly restricted to women with young children who largely accepted that reducing their working hours would be career-limiting in the context of a norm of long working hours that is profession-wide. The need for more attention to issues of work–personal life integration and flexible working had been identified by HR and by some of the partners (senior management) in the firm, although other partners were rather sceptical about this.

Action researchers were brought in to Proffirm by a woman partner in the firm working with HR to look at these issues. The research team were externally sponsored as part of a larger research project. Although senior partners did not initiate this change project, they agreed, in principle, to support the process as there was no cost to the firm. However, it is significant that the "problem" was identified mainly by HR and not by top management, most of whom did not see work–personal life integration as an issue in their own personal lives despite working excessively long hours. Many of them were men with wives who worked either part time or not at all, supporting their husbands' careers. This articulation of the problem by senior management as one which only affected other people made it difficult to get the support necessary to allocate sufficient time to the process of transforming culture and practices. This process takes time, but short-term approaches to time emerged as a major theme in this organisation and an issue permeating the whole process. This case study therefore discusses the first stages of a dual agenda project in a professional services practice and reflects on the reasons it was not possible to take forward the organisational learning gained from the early stages of the process to bring about transformative changes in practices and culture.

THE PROCESS

After explaining the project to the senior management group, it was decided that the researchers would work collaboratively with one work team to explore working practices and their impact on both performance, articulated in terms of quality client service, and work–personal life integration of team members. The particular work team, comprising three male partners as well as male and female managers and staff, was selected for the project because it faced a number of challenges. It was a multi-specialist team, based in different locations, working to tight deadlines on a job for a major client. In addition to work throughout the year, the job involved a six-week period (including weekends) of working away from home at the client's premises under the pressure of tight deadlines. There had been a very high turnover of staff in the team in recent years, although the partners in the team were insistent that this had not caused major problems.

The researchers carried out collaborative interviews with all the members of the client-serving team, focusing on the nature and demands of the job, working practices, definitions of success, and the impact on their personal lives and on their workplace performance. These interviews allowed taboo topics to emerge and be discussed, such as the unreliability of time sheets for recording hours worked as a basis for fee charging, and helped people to start thinking about their working practices and their personal lives in different ways. Three major themes emerged from these interviews, relating to notions of professionalism, time, and flexibility and trust. These were explored in terms of related assumptions and practices that were undermining the dual agenda.

Traditional assumptions that were surfaced but not fully challenged in this case study therefore include:

- Being professional means being available to clients at all times.

- Only those professionals who are willing to be constantly available and "go the extra mile" for clients are promotable.

- Personal time must be sacrificed to give quality client service.

- Professionals cannot be trusted to get their work done unless they can be seen by managers.

- Number of hours working visibly in the workplace are an indication of how hard people are working and how productive they are.

- Not recording all hours worked makes staff look more efficient.

THEME 1. CLIENT RELATIONS, PROFESSIONALISM AND "SUPER-PLEASING" THE CLIENT

A dominant theme in all the interviews related to notions of professionalism, defined in terms of displaying appropriate behaviours, particularly constant availability to the client. Some of the interview participants talked of being driven by the imperative of what they termed "super-pleasing" the client. This was related to the idea of being willing to "go the extra mile" which was also widely discussed as an indicator of professionalism, commitment and likelihood of being promoted within the firm. Super-pleasing could include doing more than the client asked for, or fitting in with unrealistic timelines set by clients. For example, if the client did not provide information in good time, team members would have to work under pressure to provide the service within tight deadlines, often working excessively long hours. Thus, client inefficiency could impose totally unrealistic deadlines. There was a reluctance to ask clients for information earlier so that the job could be done within regular hours, as this was deemed unprofessional. Thus, personal time was sacrificed in the interests of super-pleasing the client and being "professional".

Assumptions about Working Practices

The assumptions about working practices that are optimal for the business which emerge in this theme are that being professional and providing quality client service involves:

- Working to the client's timescale.

- Not "hassling" the client for information.

- Being prepared to work long hours to demonstrate commitment to client service.

- Putting work before private life which is assumed to demonstrate caring about the client.

- Making ambitious promises to clients.

- Treating the client as a privileged member of the team with rights but not responsibilities.

All the senior members of the team talked about "strong players" as those who are prepared to do the above. By implication, those who have personal commitments that can impinge on work are not regarded as strong players in this organisation. These assumptions and the working practices which they sustained had a number of negative consequences for performance and efficiency as well as for work–personal life integration. These include the following.

Consequences for Professional Service and Work–Personal Life Integration

- Lack of control over timescales and planning, which affects efficiency.

- Frustration at not being able to get on with the job (when client does not produce information on time).

- Increased pressures to meet deadlines.

- Creates extra work.

- An overvaluing of firefighting skills (e.g., being willing and able to work all night to deal with a deadline crisis), which obscures the importance of other skills (e.g., interpersonal skills which may help to avoid the crisis).

- Reduces efficiency.

- Reduces opportunities for flexibility and work–personal life integration.

- Increases staff turnover and hence reduces continuity of client service by experienced staff.

Thus, this notion of professionalism undermines not only the ability to integrate work with personal life but also effectiveness and the ability to provide the optimum client service towards which professionalism is aimed.

THEME 2. TIME

Time was a major issue in all the interviews. It was clear that the prevailing long hours of work were sustained by norms and assumptions relating to both visible and invisible time. Paradoxically, people were being judged both by the number of hours they were visibly at the workplace and also by invisible time that was not recorded on time sheets. In theory, time sheets should make it easy to schedule and account for working hours, but there are a number of informal/cultural processes whereby a norm of longer hours is sustained in this organisation. There are both explicit rules and also implicit norms about how to complete time sheets, and often these are contradictory. The explicit rhetoric is that all work done for a particular client's job must be charged to that client, to ensure that this is reflected in billing. The informal norm, however, is that any hours which are in excess of what has been charged in the budget will not be recorded. Thus, internalisation of the high standards of professionalism can result in extra hours of work which are then regarded as a "choice" rather than a reflection of heavy workloads or unrealistic budgets.

Assumptions about Working Practices

The assumptions about working practices that related to time were:

- Working hours can be accurately recorded (although the interviews revealed that this was not the case).

- It is unprofessional to record all hours worked when the budget is tight.

- Staff will work as long as it takes to get a job done.

- If hours were not recorded people could not be trusted to do the work.

- Hours worked represents effort and productivity.

- Time sheets are necessary to provide quality client service and to remain competitive.

- Not recording all working hours makes people look more efficient and enhances promotion opportunities.

- Making all work visible would create legal and other problems.

The budget to which the project team was working was extremely tight, though considered to be necessary to retain the client in a competitive market. All team members admitted to working longer hours than those they recorded to make sure the job was completed—that is, they worked invisible hours. This was even the case for the more junior staff who earned overtime for hours worked beyond their contracted hours. It included, for example, doing extra work at night in their hotel room during the six-week period at the client's premises. This was constructed as a choice, but there was a view that recording all the hours they worked would make them look inefficient as well as unprofessional. Although the senior managers claimed not to know about the invisible work undertaken to support tight budgets, they accepted that some invisible work was a way of creating an image of super-efficiency. Again, there are consequences for the dual agenda.

Consequences

The business issues included:

- Some work becomes invisible because it is not recorded.

- Consequently, it is difficult to estimate accurately how long a job takes and therefore budgets may be unrealistic.

- The focus may be on number of hours put into a job rather than outcomes.

- Impact on billing and efficiency.

- Long-term impact of long working hours on retention.

These interact with personal life issues:

- Long working hours limits time for other activities.
  - Time for personal life is sacrificed.
  - Opportunities for flexibility (e.g., associated with peaks and troughs of work) are obscured.

THEME 3. FLEXIBILITY AND TRUST

Given the concern with professionalism and the common practice of working more hours than are recorded, it was surprising to find that there was a low level of trust in the team with regard to flexible forms of work. Managers felt they had to manage by what they called "doing the wander" (walking around) in order to see that everybody was working and there was a view that people might not be trusted to work at home or flexibly because they could not be monitored in this way. This is exacerbated by the belief in the need for constant availability to the client. The assumptions underpinning these practices were closely linked with those relating to the two preceding themes. There were many peaks and troughs in workload, but the assumptions about the need for constant staff availability and visibility in the workplace meant that they were expected to be at their desks even in less busy times. In less busy times, they could find themselves bored and pass the time by, for example, surfing the Internet. Managers would then come round, see that they were not working and feel that their suspicions about not being able to trust staff to get on with their work independently were confirmed. So, there was a vicious circle of overwork, inflexibility and lack of trust. At busy times, interruptions by managers could prevent staff from getting on with their work and reduce efficiency.

Assumptions about Working Practices

- It is necessary to be available to the client at all times.

- Staff should be seen to be working, even at less busy times.

- Staff cannot be trusted to work well if they are not observed/monitored.

- Staff may not "put in the hours" if they work flexibly.

- Some working hours are more valuable than others—for example, people who worked late were valued more than those who came in early and left early.

- Flexibility is only required by women with young children.

- Flexibility in working time is one-way rather than mutual (flexibility is regarded as a favour given to staff but it is not recognised that they can be flexible in return to meet business needs).

- Work–personal life integration is not an issue for strong players (and hence this has to be sacrificed to succeed in this firm).

Consequences

- Long working hours.

- Reluctance to experiment with innovative ways of working.

- Frequent monitoring (due to low trust) can reduce undisturbed time to get on with work.

- Lack of undisturbed time is inefficient.

- Lack of opportunities for flexibility at less busy times is bad for morale and can make people look unproductive, reinforcing lack of trust—for example, if staff have to be present in the office in less busy times they may have little work to do and be labelled as idle by managers.

- There is a feeling that personal life is not valued.

- The integration of work with personal life is difficult.

- Retention problems.

Feedback and Discussion: The Round Table Meeting

These emergent themes and ideas were discussed with participants as the collaborative interviews progressed: pushing their understandings of professionalism and client service; questioning the practice of setting budgets according to the number of hours a job takes, despite the recognition that time sheets were unreliable; and challenging participants to consider what it would take to be able to trust team members to work flexibly in their own time or place. These were micro-interventions which provided opportunities to work with members of the team to reflect on these issues before the feedback or round table session in which the researchers and the work team discussed the themes together, including the emerging assumptions and consequences.

The team expressed surprise that, although all the issues had consequences for work–personal life integration, there were a greater number of negative consequences for organisational performance and professional service and this was an incentive to think about change. Inevitably, there was some initial resistance to ideas about the need for change, especially from the partners, but also from members of the team who were initially reluctant to question so many basic assumptions underpinning their everyday practice. Much of the resistance was framed in terms of the need to be competitive. For example, there was a view that if they did not "super-please" the client, the client would go elsewhere. However, by the end of this two-hour meeting some of the team were beginning to engage with and reflect upon the notion that it might be possible to give better client service by changing the nature of the relationship, while also making work more predictable and enhancing work–personal life integration.

Some ideas were easier for the team to think about constructively than others. Most of their ideas for change were related to the theme of flexibility and trust and there were some innovative ideas about how to change patterns and places of work and encourage trust. The notion that the client might be treated as one of the team and more openly involved in planning to avoid last minute deadlines and enhance the overall client service was also considered. Issues about recording working time, however, were considered to be more difficult. The issue of recording all time on official time sheets was considered a huge problem, but one which is endemic across the profession and, therefore, they felt that at this stage it was unrealistic to try and change unilaterally. The majority view was that changing time sheets would increase vulnerability and risk of losing clients. One partner, however, raised the possibility that this could be an opportunity to be leading edge, setting a trend.

Overall, it was felt that there was a hierarchy of issues to be addressed and changes which could be aimed for. There was a view that small wins need to be achieved first, before tackling more problematic issues, and that flexibility and trust would need to be considered before the issues of client relations and time, which fundamentally undermine work–personal life integration, could be addressed.

The micro-interventions realised through the collaborative interviews and the feedback/round table session raised awareness of counter-productive assumptions that undermine effectiveness and work–personal life integration and demonstrated the connectedness of the two aspects of the dual agenda, though not all members of the team had taken these issues on board. After the feedback meeting the team were moving towards a position where they may have collaborated with the research team in initiating an action research experiment addressing one of the themes. The next steps would have been to engage further with resistance displayed by some team members and to collaboratively explore new ways of working, taking account of the dual agenda find-ings and developing a pilot "experiment". Such an experiment would have enabled them to experience for themselves what it feels like to work in different ways. However, management were reluctant to spend more time on this issue or to consider that investment of some time at this stage could save time in the future. The time constraints were, of course, integral to and symptomatic of the issues raised in this process. Thus, the process had begun to raise awareness of these issues among this team, but without allocating sufficient time and resources to follow though the process and implement changes to improve performance.

At a later date, free consultancy money was used to bring in consultants to work with two different teams in the organisation, but again the initiative came from HR while senior management remained sceptical about the problems or need for change. So, there was limited motivation to pursue the very challenging dual agenda issues that emerged from the pilot work.

This project does demonstrate the possibilities for using this method with this time-squeezed professional group to challenge systemic barriers to work–personal life integration as well as optimum performance. However, it also illustrates the importance of the acknowledgement of a problem or need by top management and commitment to take action to resolve the problems. Without this perspective there will not be sufficient motivation to undertake or support others in the organisation in undertaking the intensive change process.

Proffirm therefore remained at the elaboration stage of action learning. There were formal work–life policies, but no attempt to use flexibility to innovate and transform the organisation. Moreover, the predominance among senior management of men with supportive, non-career wives obscured any sense of gender injustice, even though the assumptions surfaced in this process were clearly gendered. That is, the characteristics and skills that were valued were those manifested by people who were able to spend elastic time in the workplace without worrying about other commitments. Moreover, the "macho" skills of firefighting and working in crisis mode were valued more than interpersonal skills and crisis prevention. This was illustrated graphically by one manager who said that he had an excellent senior woman manager, but when it came to staying all night to get work finished, she just could not do it; so, her career advancement would be limited. He was reluctant to look at the reason work crises arose.

LESSONS LEARNED FROM THIS CASE STUDY

- It is difficult to initiate change unless a problem or need is clearly identified and agreed upon by top management and across the organisation or teams involved.

- HR alone is unlikely to have the power and resources to sponsor intensive change processes with a commitment to go beyond learning to action to bring about change.

- Change occurs more readily when participants can identify personally with the problem at some level, as this releases energy and motivation for creative thinking.

- There are a number of assumptions in this professional practice context that undermine the dual agenda—particularly, professional, time and trust issues which undermine performance and work–personal life integration.

- Raising taboo issues and surfacing deeply held values and assumptions and examining their impact on the dual agenda are essential but not sufficient for fundamental and sustainable learning and change to take place.

- There can be deep resistance to recognising the gendered nature of counterproductive assumptions.

- There is a need to build on the learning that takes place about the impact of counterproductive assumptions and working practices on the dual agenda by collaborative brainstorming about possible solutions and innovations for change and experimenting with new approaches.

- Real change takes time, although time invested can save time in the long term by reducing inefficient practices. There are no quick fixes.

CHAPTER 5

Printco

A small business with its back against the wall

It is often argued that small businesses cannot undertake change to support work–personal life integration because there is less scope (e.g., for covering absent staff) and fewer resources, although in fact evidence suggests that smaller firms are often more, rather than less, flexible in terms of working time and other innovations than their larger competitors (Dex & Schreibl, 2001). Indeed, some of the best examples of workplace flexibility come from medium and small enterprises. The resources issue is largely irrelevant when looking at changing working practices rather than thinking in terms of "benefits", such as childcare.

As with larger firms, successful change process initiatives can meet a dual agenda of enhancing both organisational effectiveness and work–life integration of employees in small- and medium-sized firms. Printco is a good example of this. In this case the change agent was not external but a new managing director who challenged existing taken-for-granted assumptions about how things should be done and worked collaboratively with the workforce to develop mutual flexibility of working time and practices including functional flexibility that enabled the company to grow. In doing so they turned around the fortunes of what had previously been an ailing company as well as meeting employees' personal needs.

THE COMPANY

Printco is a small non-unionised company based in central England, manufacturing labels and nameplates using screen-printing, engraving and vinyl graphics. The current managing director joined the company at a time when it had ten years of losses behind it. He recognised that change was essential—another 12 months of performing in the same way and the company would have folded. As the MD put it:

> We had a "backs to the wall" situation but in some ways that's good for bringing about change.

In contrast with the views expressed in many organisations that work–personal life integration is a cost rather than a strategy and can only be considered in times of financial security, it was the very economic difficulties that provided a context for innovation and transformation.

At this time the culture was one in which all decisions were made from the top allowing no collaboration from the workers themselves. Not only did this fail to build on the expertise of those who did the work, but it also meant that no strategic decisions were taken, as top management was too busy making day-to-day decisions, which could have been more effectively delegated. There was also a culture of one person one job (rather than multi-skilling), which undermined flexibility, and there was high absenteeism and turnover of staff. Working practices (rigid work hours and specialisms) which made it difficult for employees to integrate work and personal life were thus also undermining the business.

This presented a challenge, which the MD regarded as an opportunity, and the precarious state of the firm was used as a lever for change. The *first assumptions that he challenged* were that:

- Personal life issues can only be taken into account when there are good financial resources.

- Employees need to be "managed" and cannot contribute to strategic or day-to-day decision making.

- Employees cannot be trusted to do what is best for the firm, without constant management.

- Maintaining job boundaries is important.

INTRODUCING CHANGE: LISTENING AND COLLABORATING

Interestingly, in this case the changes were not deliberately driven by work–personal life integration or work–life balance issues from the outset, but rather by business concerns. Only later did the company learn that these were the terms currently used to describe the dual agenda approach that actually developed. The MD admitted:

> It wasn't driven by a Mr Nice Guy approach to it. I mean it just so happens that ... we can get a win–win situation out of it and I mean all the objections to work–life balance or work–life integration are because people are seeing it as an imposition as opposed to an opportunity. And, you know, it was only when someone came up to give a talk to local business people about work–life balance that we knew (what we were doing) had a name to be perfectly honest.

In order to bring about changes, the MD found ways of involving and collaborating with the workforce. This included holding briefing sessions on the state of the business and the need for change, telling them that:

> ... if we didn't pull together then ... we'd all be out of a job

as well as walking round and talking to and getting to know people. In these conversations he was not only finding out about their jobs but also about their lives generally—bringing in personal as well as job-related matters. This mirrors the process of legitimising personal as well as organisational issues, setting the scene for dual agenda solutions. The process therefore had parallels with collaborative interactive action research (CIAR) but rather than an external person looking at the taken-for-granted practices, the new MD brought an external perspective. He was able to do this because he did not come from the printing industry. So, if he wanted to know how to do a job he had to ask the workers themselves—a process similar to the sharing of expertise that is crucial to the CIAR process described in Chapter 2. He made it clear that he did not know anything about printing and therefore needed employees' collaboration, but he did know how to run a company. So, together they could collaborate to come up with new ideas to save the business. People were enthused about having the opportunity to input and started to feel engaged and feel more valued because they were asked for their opinion.

Collaborating for Mutual Flexibility

The starting point for enhancing performance and, as it turned out, work–personal life integration was to introduce multi-skilling. When multi-skilling was first introduced some of the workers agreed that they would buy into that but asked about having some flexibility of working hours in return. Thus, the dual agenda presented itself, because personal life concerns were listened to and valued. Multi-skilling provided opportunities for flexibility and gradually new ways of working evolved.

There were already some part-time workers and others working shifts which were very regularised, but some workers wanted to have slightly different hours (e.g., to fit in with bus timetables or lifts home). Listening to what workers wanted revealed the potential for two-way flexibility—to benefit the workers and the business. From this starting point the firm has now developed to the point where there are 26 different working patterns within the 38-people workforce. Full time in production is 39 hours a week, but there are various different start and finishing times. Almost any arrangement is accommodated: compressed working week, part time, term time only, variable part time, home-working and extended lunch break. There are part-timers doing between 8 and 32 hours a week. New employees are encouraged to discuss their flexibility needs at their final interview, and existing employees who want to change their hours are encouraged to propose a solution.

This predated new legislation in Britain, which gives employees the right to ask for a change in working hours, but goes further in that employees are asked to propose a solution having talked to their colleagues first. The onus is on the employee to discuss things with their workmates, and then say how the proposed changes in working arrangements will work so that it benefits everyone. There are no formal procedures, unlike the recommendations of the new legislation. The MD feels that formal procedures would kill creativity. Rather, flexibility is totally accomplished at an informal level.

Because flexibility is regarded as a strategic opportunity for engaging employees and enhancing the business there are no judgements about the validity of the reasons for wishing to work flexibly. These are not limited to family reasons nor is it primarily women who want to work differently. Some people have a one-off need to change their working pattern (e.g., if it is someone's birthday or they want to go away for the weekend). Others want to change patterns for a longer period for family or other reasons:

> We have a dad who works two days one week and three days the next and his wife is the main breadwinner. So, you know, that's the other thing, we never actually ask. **If someone wants to change their working pattern we don't ask why.** They always tell you, you can't stop them telling you, but we don't restrict it to those with caring responsibilities. I mean one has an extended lunch break, goes down the gym and another has got her horse, you know her time off it's not the orthodontist for the child, it's for the horse.

The important point is that leadership has encouraged a culture in which employees come to management and propose a solution rather than just presenting a problem. By being open to these ideas the firm *capitalises on employees' creative thinking.* Flexibility of working patterns, methods and time is regarded as an opportunity for innovation and organisational learning is transformational.

Similarly, there are no jobs for which flexibility will not be sought. Even jobs that are assumed to be necessarily full time can be adapted in this context. This enables the firm to address employees' changing needs over the life cycle. For example, it was taken for granted that a facilitator working with the printers must be working full time. The innovative post of facilitator is someone who does the preparation and provides support to enable printers to work to full capacity on their machines, as explained below:

> If you've four machines and you've got four printers—that's one way of operating and they do that they have a fifth person to go and fetch this stuff, you know they spend a lot of time finding things, or you can have three printers and one person facilitating. And now you think I only get three-quarters of the output, but you don't. You actually get more than you did with four. That's convention out of the window again you see. **But, what you're doing is actually doing more preparatory work and making sure that the three people who are printing are able to be printing more at the time.** There's a lot of waste time either looking for the screen or mixing the ink up and things like that and if someone can actually make sure that all the bits, the information, the screen, the material, the ink, are there.

However, one facilitator wanted to work part time four days a week with a fixed day off. She talked to the printers to see if that would work out. They all agreed that if she did certain bits of preparation before she went home on the night before she had her day off, that would cover it adequately; so, she changed to a four-day week. And then her partner changed his job and he had to work weekends, so she asked for a variable day off. She changed her hours again later to fit in with other life changes and each time the team was able to accommodate this. So, valued staff were retained and productivity sustained or improved.

Because of the ethos of mutual trust and reciprocity among the workforce, flexibility is enhanced, including cross-traditional boundary cover—another spin-off from multi-skilling. For example, there was a situation where there were only two people in the sales office at lunchtime, so if the phones rang then the accounts office covered this. This mirrors the collaboration and cover that was developed between sales and service in the Xerox case.

As new flexible practices are developed and tried out they are docu-
mented, but are regarded as business practices not HR systems:

> ... we tend to try things out and what works we then adopt as a practice
> and write our procedures around it. **Never write a procedure before
> you've got a practice.** And even within that we do have an employee
> handbook even for our size of company, but we don't actually have a
> checklist of work–life balance opportunities.

The changes are regarded as integral to the business and not just
marginal HR issues.

> It's an integrated approach and it's not even an integrated approach to
> HR, it's the way we run our business; so, it's an integrated way of running
> a business, part of that is flexible working. Flexible working is about
> multi-skilling, on the one hand, which we had to do, and flexibility in
> terms of how we can treat people.

There are many benefits of this new approach to the business as well as
employees' personal lives. The engagement of employees with business
aims, mutual flexibility and collaboration were also encouraged by self-
managed teams, which enabled the firm to capitalise on opportunities
for expansion. This could result in teams deciding to work longer for
specific business-led reasons, For example, the MD explained:

> About three or four years ago we set up the vinyl cut department or vinyl
> graphics department ... just was two people initially, just like a little self-
> managed team looking after everything from their own graphics, doing
> their own estimating, in fact right through to inspection and packing. And
> that was a good example because suddenly an opportunity arose ...
> where we had to quadruple output in two months. So, again (I went) to
> them and said, "Well, this is an opportunity and it's also a threat because
> if we don't do it, then not only will we lose that opportunity but we'll lose
> the business we had before." And they came back the next day and said,
> "We'll work seven days a week for two months and if it carries on after
> that we'll take somebody else on." And, they said, "This is the equipment
> we need, this is the space we need." So, we just worked out, they sorted it
> all out and they did it and they quadrupled it.

Hence, flexibility clearly worked to the firm's advantage in this scenario. But, it was again only possible because of the culture of mutual trust and collaboration. In fact, this team of two did work seven days a week for two months, after which the firm took on a third person to bolster the team.

MUTUAL TRUST

The underlying philosophy of the company is to trust people until they prove themselves untrustworthy rather than the other way around. Trust and reciprocity are essential to the process:

You have to believe and trust in people ... That's your starting point really. If you don't trust your people then it won't work. So, things like home-working, if you're going to ring up every five minutes, won't work. But, if you actually want people to use their brains as well as their brawn, then you've got to treat them fairly. And its all part of the give and take that makes it work because if people feel it's all give on their part, then they're not going to be willing to carry on doing it. If they can see, yes, we get something out of it and the company gets something out of it, then everybody is content and drives it forward and it actually gathers momentum as time goes on.

The MD reckons that it took about 18 months to build up the sort of mutual trust necessary to make this work, because workers had not previously been informed that the company was not doing very well, and they had to get used to a very different, more open style of management.

Inevitably, there may be some who may abuse trust but this can be dealt with within the system, encouraging honesty and mutually beneficial solutions:

If they're persistently not doing their hours, then we have a chat with them and say, "Do you want to renegotiate your hours?" or "How are you going to make (the time) up?" But, generally, people do it of their own volition, even to the point where one of the printers was off absent one day and I said to him the next morning, "What was wrong with you?"

And, he said, "To be perfectly honest I had a hangover." I said, "Well, it's not a very good reason for paying you is it?" And, he said, "No," and I said, "Well, how about making your hours up over the next two weeks then?" And, he said, "Fair dos."

In most cases however, when workers want flexibility for any of a whole range of reasons, they work it out between themselves, covering for each other and reaching equitable arrangements. So, there is no need to "*throw a sickie*", as one person expressed it, because there are ways of working out flexibility needs without pretending to be ill.

Trust extends to encouraging and supporting innovation and training and developing people to do this, which has helped the business to grow:

... people on the shop floor, they try ideas out and sometimes they work, sometimes they don't. And you have to have this, get them into the way of thinking that they're not going to get told off if it doesn't work. They've got to learn from the mistakes and move on. If people make the same mistake time and time again, then of course it's an issue as it would be in any business. But, it is a case of trusting people, training and developing them well. We've put a lot of time and money into training and development of individuals.

Consequently, there is a willingness to try new ideas and take risks, together with an acceptance that inevitably not all work out. Staff empowerment is actively encouraged through open communication, delegation and team working as well as training. At one point, a grade of innovator was introduced to encourage those who wanted to experiment. Rather than having to be promoted out of their jobs to get on, they introduced the concept of an innovator as somebody who challenges the status quo and could get a pay increase.

Resistance

There was inevitably some initial resistance to change but it was largely based on the assumptions that multi-skilling might erode the value of people's skills and that opportunities for flexible working time arrangements were only applicable to certain people. As a new understanding of opportunities for various forms of flexibility was agreed upon in terms of mutual benefits available to everyone for any reason, people became enthusiastic about this idea.

Line managers are often major barriers to the effectiveness of flexible working arrangements, particularly in larger organisations. Most of the line managers at Printco could see the advantages of the various forms of flexibility, but one was somewhat ambivalent. He could see the two sides. On the one hand, it might make his life easier in some respects if the work was more regularised. On the other hand, he knows that there is now virtually no absenteeism and turnover of staff since moving towards more flexible working schedules. This ambivalence comes from working in a culture where regular working hours are the norm and it is assumed the most effective way of working. When this is questioned, however, it becomes apparent that flexibility actually extends the working day, with some people coming in from 6 a.m. and some leaving a bit later in the evenings so that flexible working arrangements have business as well as personal benefits.

Systemic Change

The process has involved systemic change throughout the firm, including a movement towards different management and organisational structures, which involves giving people opportunities to develop within their speciality, often in self-managed teams, without having to move away from the shop floor to administrative managerial posts:

> *Rather than looking at it as a normal management hierarchical structure, we try to give people opportunities to develop either by having these little self-managed teams where people are still very hands-on but taking responsibility for organising it, or other ways of giving them some challenges and being able to reward them for it.* **So, we've moved away from sort of standard organisational structures.**

The process has also included looking at working hours and encouraging a focus on work done rather than hours worked. This has included cutting down on overtime. If people were systematically working overtime the nature of the job was examined and often a new person taken on. Of course, this could mean that some employees would lose income, but they have found win–win solutions for this too, as the MD explained, saying:

> *"I do understand the fact that you're perhaps doing (overtime) partially to boost your income; I'm not daft. What I'll do is pay you what I've been paying you (with overtime) for a basic week. . . . If you can do your work in 39 hours you can still have the money, but you owe me six hours if we need it." And, of course, you know, you can imagine what the result was. In a very short period of time they managed to do it in 39 hours. So, the company's no worse off. It's actually made it easier to get the basic pay up to more acceptable levels. So, again, it comes against this present argument that people should be paid for how many hours they're there. It's payment for what you achieve. And, in fact, **we actually make a saving because we don't actually have to have anyone in on a Saturday morning and pay the lighting bill for it.***

The process is underpinned by a particular management style, involving trust and the ability to collaborate and be flexible, although this MD retains strategic responsibility:

> *. . . my role largely is far more supportive than it is managing, although it's sort of moved a little bit recently towards setting the strategy and saying this is where we want to get to, and this is what we've got to achieve. The "how" is up to negotiation. You know, so rather than actually going the whole hog, we do involve people in the strategy. But, at the end of the day, you know, if you are the managing director you have to bite the bullet. Having listened to people you have to decide what the direction is.*

The general people-oriented approach of collaboration, trust and problem-solving towards win–win solutions has also generalised to relationships with customers and suppliers which has benefited the business:

> *Customers . . . we work with people. We're there to . . . we try to provide them with solutions to the problems to try to take some of their problems away from them. So, in terms of elimination of problems, yes, we do take a similar approach with our customers (as staff) . . . We want to be solutions providers, but we're also at the same time, you know, as I said, quite clearly an ethical company. By that we mean we will be*

trustworthy to employees, suppliers, customers, anybody else ... Six years ago, seven years ago when you wanted to buy something, you know, you shopped around every time, there was no loyalty to suppliers. Now we have regular suppliers ...we're loyal to them and they repay that. ... So, again, working with people ... it's trying to find ways that are not even win-neutral, you know, we try for win–win.

COULD THE LESSONS LEARNED FROM THIS COMPANY BE APPLIED TO A LARGER COMPANY?

The main difference from the approaches commonly taken in larger companies, where work–personal life integration initiatives tend to come from HR rather than being seen as central strategic issues, is that changing practices are worked out before establishing policy. Most larger companies tend to develop policies first and then try to put them into practice, often with limited success.

For this approach to work in larger organisations, the MD suggests it will be necessary to work with smaller units or departments, as in the Xerox case, and then diffuse the experiences more widely:

If a large company is considered as a series of small departments, yes. And I suppose the only difference really between a large and a small one is in a small one you can set the culture easier and have a more hands-on approach. In a large company you've got to win the hearts and minds of the line managers before you can implement it across an organisation.

SUMMARY OF OUTCOMES/EVALUATION

*Yes, I mean the company is profitable. And, you know, yes it's an upper quartile performance for our industry sector now. **Now productivity or sales per head are over 200% greater** than what it was six years ago.*

The process and the consequent changes in working practices and culture have brought clear business benefits, enhanced performance and, arguably, ensured survival. Outcomes include:

- *Profitability has increased **from break-even in 1996 to an average of £85k per annum over the last three years with roughly the same number of staff.** Since 1996 manufacturing turnover per FTE has doubled. **With more delegation and innovation, the performance of other aspects of production has improved.** Wastage rates have more than halved.*

- ***Industry data show that** the company is now performing in the upper quartile of the industry—**profit, as a % of turnover was 8% for Printco in 2001 compared with an average for the sector of 1.6%. In 1996 profits were virtually zero.***

- *Significantly improved job satisfaction **has been a major contributor to staff retention levels, which are very high.***

- *Absenteeism rates are down **from five to six days per annum to two to three. Staff are more interested in their job, happier with their work— personal life integration, more engaged in what they do and how that relates to the performance of the business.** It represents a move away from presenteeism to genuine engagement.*

- ***Many of the new business ideas and innovations come from individuals in the company.***

- ***Printco Products is perceived as a good company to work for.** Recruitment is easier. **Pay is no longer a major motivator (though the company has increased pay levels from below average to average local rates).** Other things being equal, flexible working gives Printco Products an edge in a tightening labour market.*

In fact, when we have a vacancy we usually get someone recommended by one of our existing staff. They must feel that it's a good company to work for. We pay about average for the area, not over the top. But, people don't leave; they very rarely leave:

- ***The company's new attitude to customer service, enabled by all of the changes brought in since 1996, has dramatically improved the quality of the customer base and the extent of repeat business.** Average order sizes have increased—key for productivity improvement.*

- *The total flexibility also makes it easier to adapt to statutory rights, such as parental leave, because of the willingness of colleagues to be involved in working out solutions. Again this is viewed as an opportunity for change and innovative working patterns have resulted, meeting the dual agenda of workplace effectiveness and work–personal life integration.*

- *The work–personal life integration benefits are enormous, as employees know they can work out solutions to work–personal life issues as and when their lives change. Employees also benefit in many ways from the firm's success. For example, if the firm had closed down some employees had mortgages that they would have been unable to pay, resulting in the feeling that their "houses were on the line".*

LESSONS LEARNED FROM THIS CASE STUDY

- Organisational change to meet a dual agenda of work–personal life integration and workplace effectiveness is possible in small- and medium-sized organisations and in the manufacturing sector. Limited human and financial resources need not be barriers to transformational organisational learning.

- Systemic change can be easier in small businesses or smaller units within larger organisations than in big firms.

- Someone coming into a senior position from outside the organisation can act as a change agent by questioning assumptions and practices that internal people may take for granted. Total outsiders, however, are not embedded in the power system and may lack organisation-wide influence, unlike a new leader or in this case a managing director.

- Financial difficulties, often regarded as barriers to change can actually be levers for effective change to meet a dual agenda.

- Working practices which make it difficult for employees to integrate work and personal life can also undermine organisational effectiveness.

- Being open about the state of the business, involving employees in problem-solving and legitimising personal concerns creates a context where creative dual agenda solutions can be developed.

- Multi-skilling can be a catalyst for two-way flexibility.

- When employees are involved in decision making they are enthused, feel engaged and valued.

- When employees are encouraged to present flexible solutions rather than asking for flexible working as a "favour" they problem-solve with colleagues and can be creative in developing arrangements with win–win consequences.

- If flexibility is regarded as a business strategy rather than a "favour" the reasons for employees seeking flexibility becomes unimportant and there is a willingness to look for flexible alternative working arrangements in a wide range of jobs.

- Practices are more important than policies for bringing about change. If policies are to be developed they should be based on experiences in practice rather than vague intentions.

- Mutual trust is at the heart of the change process, crucial to flexibility and innovation, but takes time to develop.

- Some pockets of resistance are inevitable but can be worked with by addressing underlying assumptions, demonstrating fairness and favourable business as well as personal outcomes.

- The process involves systemic change—including changes in culture (e.g., regarding working hours and management and promotional structures).

- The process can be generalised to some extent to the ways an organisation works with other stakeholders, such as customers and suppliers, with benefits to the business.

- Outcomes of the change process include enhanced performance, productivity and profitability, greater employee satisfaction and enhanced work–personal life integration.

CHAPTER 6

Recruitco

Culture and practice development in a small business: support from top management is essential but not sufficient

BACKGROUND

Recruitco is a small recruitment company with around 40 employees, specialising in the IT sector. The business depends on being able to attract, develop and retain good, well-qualified graduates. As the company is located within the commuter belt for London there is a need to compete against London firms by being perceived as a good place to work. The chief executive, who founded the firm more than 20 years ago, has always recognised the importance of developing, supporting and empowering her staff. She implicitly accepted that what is good for employees is also good for business. As in the case of Printco this was not initially articulated as work–life integration but simply as good management practice that recognises that families and society are changing and that traditional management styles that value only workers who have no responsibilities or interests beyond work will not be effective. As the years have passed the culture and practice of valuing and acknowledging staff has developed with a range of innovative and supportive practices. However, despite this supportive context and recognition of the dual agenda, attempts to introduce a change in working practices, initially by encouraging informal trust-based flexible working arrangements, had run into difficulties. This case study explores the process whereby a small business that already recognised the importance of work–life integration was able to develop its working practices systematically, to better meet the needs of both employees and the business. Significant elements of the existing supportive culture and practices, prior to the change process included:

- An extensive training programme so that staff can be empowered to do their work and do not have to be constantly monitored.

- An extensive induction programme to understand everyone's role.

- A culture of celebrating good work and thanking people rather than taking employee efforts for granted. Practices range from small gestures and rituals to award schemes for outstanding employees (two nominated by staff and one by management).

- Regular team-building activities, including an annual charity focus and fund-raising event involving the entire workforce.

- All staff are entitled to a day's leave on or immediately after their birthday.

- Six-monthly appraisals, including analysis of training needs, with performance measured by deliverables. So, in theory at least, output rather than input of time was already used to assess performance and commitment.

- Informal flexibility.

The nature of the work often involved long or atypical working hours; for example, recruitment candidates often cannot be interviewed during the working day because they cannot take time off from their current jobs, so evening work is inevitable for some of the staff. However, under the informal system, if employees worked late for any reason, they often asked for time off the next day and this was generally accepted by management. The chief executive focused on the importance of getting the job done and meeting customers' needs (output) rather than hours of work (input):

I don't believe in a nine to five regime, it's irrelevant. Its getting the job done.

In this context it was expected that informal flexible working practices would be highly effective. Nevertheless, there were a number of problems with this informal system, relating to the perceived equity and fairness of the informal practices:

- Flexibility was not always linked to outputs (i.e., it was not based on mutual responsibility and trust). Some staff who were working flexibly were perceived by their colleagues to be not pulling their weight and this led to feelings of unfairness and associated backlash. It was not managers but peers who felt that some staff were abusing the informal flexibility. Staff had not had the opportunities to collaborate in the process of moving towards informally flexible working arrangements.

- Flexibility was individually negotiated between managers and staff, but there was often a lack of consistency in practice. Some managers were perceived to be showing favouritism.

- Sometimes, when staff were allowed to work flexibly, no cover was arranged, so employees had to cover for their colleagues.

The company had been struggling to make informal flexibility work for many years before the change process was introduced.

ASSUMPTIONS CHALLENGED BY THE CHANGE PROCESS

- A commitment to supporting and empowering staff and rituals to demonstrate that employees are valued is sufficient to ensure the success of informal flexibility.

- Flexibility is an individual issue, to be negotiated between employees and managers, rather than an organisational issue.

- Staff cannot organise their own flexibility or ensure that work is completed and cover maintained.

- Management must retain discretion about flexible working.

- Systematic flexibility will cost money.

- Systematic flexibility will not work in a small business.

PROCESS

The process of change at Recruitco enabled the management team to succeed in developing organisational structures and practices in line with their espoused values of employee support and empowerment, which, in turn, were recognised as essential for recruiting and retaining staff in a highly competitive labour market.

The process was facilitated by UK Government funding from the Department of Trade & Industry (DTI) Challenge Fund. This is a resource to help employers to develop and implement "work–life balance strategies" that benefit the business, customer and employee by providing researchers/consultants to work with individual companies on their specific needs. This funding was used at Recruitco to develop and enhance existing practices by an explicit focus on the process of change and development.

From the outset the process involved the workforce in the development of the flexible working system. The external researchers/consultants worked with groups of employees across the entire company on what they thought needed to be improved. This involved confronting taboo issues, such as perceived favouritism amongst managers, and challenging assumptions about flexible working. What emerged from these group discussions was a desire for a formal flexitime system. The groups were then involved in development of the parameters for this system, including consideration of how it would be managed and how it would work in practice in the company. This resulted in what staff felt was a transparent system, perceived as more equitable than the informal system. Because the whole workforce had been involved there was a commitment to making the new system work.

The formal system that emerged from this process included:

- Self-managed teams with responsibility for ensuring that work is done and customers are covered. For example, if a team member is off work for a half-day the team ensures that there is cover. Management do not have to be involved in this process. As a senior manager explained:

We let them get on with it and we haven't had any problems. It's just so much easier.

This involves:

- Two-way flexibility. Team members work to provide flexibility for individual members' needs while also ensuring that the needs of the business are met at all times.

- An official computerised flexitime system. Staff manage the computer system and cover themselves and do not have to ask managers for permission to vary hours of work.

- A buddy system. Each member of staff is paired with a buddy who knows all about each others' jobs so that they can cover for each other if they are not at work.

RESISTANCE

There was some initial resistance to these ideas from management who feared that it would create extra work for them and be difficult to manage. A number of steps were taken to address this:

- The researchers ran workshops where this resistance could be confronted and challenged. They used vignettes to explore how flexibility would be managed and how it could be handled differently. The pros and cons of a formal computerised system were explored.

- Nevertheless, some resistance remained, based on assumptions that flexible working arrangements were "favours" that some staff do not deserve. So, it was decided that the formal system would be related to performance. That is, staff who were below target were not allowed to take flexi days. This stemmed from a lack of understanding of the principles of flexibility tied to responsibility, and reluctance by some managers to move towards a fully trust-based system. In fact, the new system resulted in a very driven set of people. With flexibility, trust and responsibility they worked harder and underperformance was not an issue. This outcome was very effective in overcoming assumptions that people will not do their work effectively if they do not work standard hours.

- The chief executive and research team decided that the formal initiative would also be introduced very slowly to get doubters on board. First, it was implemented with administrative staff for a three-month pilot period and this enabled the company to iron out minor problems, learn how it all worked and what might need to be done slightly differently. It was then introduced across the sales group for another three-month pilot. This was more complex as the sales team often work offsite, including substantial overseas travelling. However, the flexitime system creates a bonus for the sales team as they can now gain time if they have put in long hours travelling and working, which they can use, for example, for long lunches, sport or attending children's school plays, etc. without having to negotiate this with management.

OUTCOMES

Bottom-line benefits

It's a very tough business climate at the moment and I really believe the high morale we have makes a difference ... we are actually holding up much better than a lot of our competitors.

- A high level of trust rather than feelings of inequity that accompanied the informal version of flexitime.

- Absenteeism rate is extremely low (less than half the national average). Staff can make up for short absences via flexible working.

- Retention rates are high. There is no problem recruiting and attracting high-quality staff, despite competing with London firms. The company is recognised as a good place to work.

- In an employee survey, commissioned by an external company, with a 100% response rate, 97% of staff said Recruitco is better than most companies to work for.

- There is the flexibility to deal with personal needs, maternity, parental and adoption leaves, in line with the company's supportive values, and in excess of statutory regulations.

- There are no performance issues for managers to deal with. This is all self-managed among teams.

- Good PR. The chief executive is often invited to give talks about how and why the system and culture work and how this saves money.

CONCLUSIONS

Once again, it is important to remember that it is the process not the outcome that is significant and may be transferable to other contexts. The change process, instigated by the Challenge Fund researchers, was a catalyst to getting involvement and collaboration around an issue that was invoking feelings of inequity. The context in this company was one in which the dual agenda was acknowledged and management endeavoured to be supportive of people's non-work needs, and yet informal flexibility was not working well. The employees at this business wanted a formalised flexitime system because they perceived the existing approach as unfair. The process of collaboration, confronting taboo issues, such as favouritism amongst managers, questioning assumptions, such as the need for management discretion in relation to flexible working, collaborative problem-solving, experimentation with new approaches, and dealing with resistance, resulted in a formal computerised flexitime system supported by self-managed teams. Such a system is unlikely to be successful if just transferred to another context without going through the process, and the process may result in different outcomes in other contexts.

In terms of organisational learning it may appear that Recruitco took a step backwards in changing from an informal to a formal flexitime system, but this must be undertsood within the unique context of the firm. Employees had requested this change because of perceived inequity in the informal system, which had been developed without going through a collaborative process. The formal system developed enhanced feelings of distributive justice (fairer outcomes), procedural justice (a fairer process for developing the system) and interpersonal justice (fair treatment by managers). Flexibility continues to be viewed as an opportunity to innovate, but the collaborative process has provided a way of harnessing this innovation in a manner perceived as equitable to all. It also meets the needs of the business and provides opportunities for employees to harmonise work and personal lives. In the future it may be possible to move back to a more informal system, building on the learning that has taken place and use the process to look at other possible innovations in working practices to enhance effectiveness and employee work–personal life integration.

LESSONS LEARNED FROM THIS CASE STUDY

- Support from the top, awareness of the dual agenda and a supportive and empowering culture is a good start but is not enough to bring about a fundamental shift towards greater flexibility.

- Informal flexibility, however well intentioned, will not work without high levels of trust among colleagues and between managers and staff.

- Perceived equity is essential for the success of informal or formal flexibility. It is difficult to achieve when flexibility is treated as an individual rather than an organisational issue.

- A process of collaboration, confronting taboo issues, questioning assumptions, collaborative problem-solving, experimentation with new approaches and dealing with resistance results in solutions which are appropriate to the specific context.

- Self-managed teams and multi-skilling via a buddy system increase personal and group responsibility and enhances flexibility and performance.

- Management performance monitoring and discretion about who can work flexibly, tied to performance, become unnecessary if teams are empowered to self-manage.

- The involvement of staff at all stages of the change process ensures commitment to making change work.

- Resistance can be confronted and worked with to increase commitment to change at all levels.

- A flexible system introduced through this collaborative process has many positive outcomes for the organisation.

CHAPTER 7

Adminco

Flexibility in transition

BACKGROUND

Adminco is an administrative company serving clients within the financial services sector. Part of a larger European company, with global business, it employs approximately 800 staff in various locations in the UK. The workforce comprises mainly clerical workers, plus managers and professionals.

This case is interesting because the change process was led by a champion in HR with very minimal resources. However, Adminco differs from many other companies with HR-led initiatives in that flexible working practices were introduced within a process of collaboration, addressing changes in culture and practice. It was recognised from the outset that a collaborative change process would be much more effective than imposing flexible solutions and that practice would be more important than policy. The process also began with a focus on work itself, rather than on the needs of particular sections of the workforce, such as those with care responsibilities.

When the change process began the company was very traditional in its working practices. Employees worked nine until five, although some evening work was necessary to meet with clients and this involved paid overtime. The only flexibility in working patterns were "concessions" made to some mothers returning from maternity leave, and this created resentment among some of their colleagues. The drivers of change included financial considerations, such as possibilities of cutting costs by better usage of their expensive London premises and of reducing overtime payments. But, it was not just a cost-cutting exercise. In order to get jobs completed and meet deadlines, the company had to rely on the goodwill of staff to work non-compulsory overtime. Increased flexibility was perceived as a way of potentially bringing work that might usually take place in the evenings into regular full-time jobs, and thus enhance control, reduce voluntary overtime and ultimately enhance client service. There were also specific issues that needed to be addressed in different parts of the business. For example, there were pockets within the organisation with very high staff turnover or with problems of work overload, which impacted on the effectiveness of some departments.

Flexible working patterns were thus identified as a possible way of addressing issues of cost, efficiency, and client service and staff turnover. So, the changes were mainly business-driven and largely predetermined. In addition, however, it was recognised that staff wanted more flexible working hours. The HR manager explained that:

> We realised that in this day and age people wanted to have more flexibility in the hours that they work and have the opportunity to have times when they can be at home or not in the work environment.

So, there were seeds of a possible dual agenda from the outset, although business needs were clearly paramount. Flexibility of working patterns was identified by HR and some managers as potential tools for meeting these, although it was not clear exactly which forms of flexibility would work in different contexts. The process began with a virtually clean sheet, as there was little or no flexibility in existing working practices. In this context, the initiatives developed thus far can be regarded as stages in an evolutionary process, with potential for further development towards mutual trust-based flexibility and innovation in working practices. While some key assumptions about working practices have already been challenged, other traditional assumptions are still being addressed. The introduction of flexible working practices was embedded in a process. The case study illustrates both the success and the limitations of this approach so far and some of the learning points to emerge in the ongoing process.

Some assumptions *challenged* by this process so far, include:

- Most people would rather earn more money than have free time (and so would be reluctant to exchange paid overtime for more flexible working hours).

- Managing flexible working will be time-consuming.

- Working hours in financial services, especially in the City—the financial heart of London—must be (at least) nine to five and service organisations should not work different hours to their clients.

Traditional assumptions *still being challenged*:

- Hours in the workplace represent effort and productivity (so input is still seen as more important than output).

- Visibility of staff is regarded as crucial—managers must know who is working when.

- Staff cannot be trusted to work unless managers are there to supervise them.

THE CHANGE PROCESS

Following initial consultation with an external consultant, a project team was formed to drive the process. This included the HR director (the sponsor of the project), the HR manager who would drive the process (the champion) and the managing director and three managers from across the business that volunteered their sectors for pilot studies (the stakeholders). There were no non-managerial staff on this team, which may have restricted outcomes. The change process began with a pilot project, involving three business areas, each with very different business issues and problems, which it was thought could benefit from more flexibility. There were three different scenarios and three completely different outcomes in the pilots.

PRESENTING PROBLEMS

The first business area had a major retention issue. Employees were doing mundane and repetitive work and turnover rates were nearly 100%. Of course, this made it very difficult to be efficient, as the manager continually had to train new people. He had tried to use what were described as:

> *usual management principles of trying to coach people and encourage them to stay and giving them extra bonus and stuff like that to try and incentivize them.*

But, to no avail.

The second business area was a very large section of the business in which all employees were doing similar work. The work was characterised by peaks and troughs. There were short busy periods at certain times of year with staff often working until midnight for a period of four to six weeks and quiet periods during the rest of year. Management believed that the norm of nine to five working was inefficient and that more flexible working hours and some shift work would improve performance. There was therefore a prior agenda of trying to introduce flexibility and shift work, stemming from management rather than staff.

The final business area to participate in the pilot study had a problem of work overload. There was a particular time of every day when there was an intense amount of work to be processed and there was a need to be able to manage this more effectively.

THE PROCESS

Each area followed the same change process, managed by the project team, but the initial problems and the outcomes were very different. The solutions that were derived for each business area were specific to their contexts. Nevertheless, each case entailed the following steps:

- Communication with team → full participation throughout.

- Review existing working practices → workflow analysis, working patterns, options for reorganisation of work to increase efficiency (e.g., home-working), productivity analysis, resources available (number of full-time and part-time staff), overtime, turnover, sickness absence rates, etc.

- Summary of actions and recommendations → for example, home-working and reorganisation.

- Present summary to managers and then to their teams.

- Review the recommendations with the team and gain their feedback and ideas → ensure any issues are ironed out.

- Prepare a business case with final recommendations, including feedback from the team and a timetable of implementation.

- Implementation for trial period.

Stage 1. Communication with the Work Team

The initial meeting with each pilot work team introduced the goal of more flexibility in working hours, which was presented as an opportunity for all:

> the process starts with a communication so the first thing that we do is that we inform people that ... we're looking at flexible working and whether there are opportunities to introduce flexible working into your business area or across the business. It will take the form of a process.

It was explained that this was part of a process and that they would be invited to participate and collaborate at all stages to ensure that all their opinions were taken into account so that everyone could potentially benefit from the review and recommendations.

Stage 2. Review Existing Working Practices

This stage is crucial. It involves diagnostic work to better understand the issues for the business and for the staff in each department. The aim of this stage was to work collaboratively with staff to understand and review existing work practices—what they did, why they did it that way and what were their key delivery points, including deadlines they had to meet. There was no explicit identification and challenging of assumptions, as there were in the collaborative interactive action research (CIAR) method illustrated in Chapters 2 and 4, but there was a questioning of why work was performed in certain ways and a willingness to look for alternative practices.

A workflow analysis was developed by the work team and project team, based on an analysis of how the work comes in and out of the department, how much work there is, work patterns, peaks and troughs of work, deadlines and dependencies on other areas—for example, whether certain pieces of work could not be accomplished until another department provided information. Looking at the whole workflow analysis helped to understand current work approaches, why particular tasks were carried out at a certain time and what drives the organisation of work. It was important to establish, for example, to what extent the organisation of work was a client-driven requirement, and what options there were for reorganising the work to make it more efficient. Questions were raised, such as whether work could be done at home and at what points do workers have to be in the office? To generate a full picture of the context, information was also collected on resources available to accomplish the work (numbers of full-time and part-time staff), and rates of overtime, turnover and sickness absence rates.

The diagnostic data were then used to map out the processes and deliverables of each business area as a basis for thinking about how people could be enabled to work more flexibly and also more effectively. It was recognised that every team was undertaking different processes and had different deliverables, different deadlines, different peaks and troughs.

Stage 3. Summary of actions and recommendations

The project team then analysed the information and ideas collected and produced a summary of actions or recommendations for consideration and discussion by the work team. This was more directive than in some of the CIAR process and there was no explicit dual agenda, although collaboration was encouraged at each stage.

The same process was followed with all of the groups, but recommendations were different. Recommendations were conceived in terms of the original flexibility goals and the work analysis for each pilot area. They included, for example, home-working, the reorganisation of work, changes to work patterns—such as earlier start, later finish, different working hours on different days, nine-day fortnights as well as part-time working and job-sharing—as appropriate to different business areas.

Stages 4 and 5. Present summary to managers and then to their teams. Review the recommendations with the team and gain their feedback and ideas → to ensure any issues are ironed out

The HR manager then took the recommendations back, first to the managers and then to the whole work team to discuss and modify and come up with a plan to which they had all contributed. Team members, including managers, were encouraged to provide feedback and thoughts on the possible flexible working arrangements, how this might impact on them as individuals and as a team and any issues or concerns they might have. They were also asked whether they could see any particular issues or barriers and whether proposed flexible arrangements would cause any other issues, such as added pressure on other team members. At this stage team members often came up with ideas about how to be more flexible and effective.

It was emphasised that the proposed changes were not compulsory and people were given the option not to adopt them. For example, one recommendation was the introduction of flexible working hours to meet the needs of the business as well as individual staff, which also involved getting rid of paid overtime. In order to take account of everyone's needs and to assuage the suspicions of some employees, all were given the option to continue to work nine to five and to be able to work paid overtime if they preferred. There was no compulsion to change to the new system, although 90% did so. Despite their involvement in planning the changes, some individuals did not want to move to a different type of working arrangement because it did not suit their personal circumstances at the time; so, this was also taken into account. Ultimately, however, most of those who declined to change wanted to buy into the new system when the advantages became more evident.

Stage 6. Prepare a business case with final recommendations, including feedback from the team and a timetable of flexible working arrangements

Once the team agreed on the way forward, a business case was prepared by the HR manager with final recommendations. This included the views of and feedback from the team. It also included a full timetable of how the new flexible working arrangements would be implemented and how they would work, and specification of what every individual's role would be in those new working arrangements.

PILOT IMPLEMENTATION

Once the manager and the team approved this, the changes were introduced, initially on a three-month trial basis. Each pilot sector managed the process themselves. After this period the project group monitored how employees felt about it and how they met deadlines and fulfilled business needs. If the initiatives were deemed successful, they were formalised. Otherwise, there was a return to previous working practices. Two out of the three pilots were successful in developing mutually beneficial flexible working arrangements. The other was not successful in this respect, but this case did provide an important learning opportunity.

THE THREE PILOT GROUP OUTCOMES

The main recommendation for the first business area, with huge retention problems, was to apply new flexible working arrangements with new working hours, including, for example, the option of working a nine-day fortnight and working at home. This was adopted by the staff and has been both popular and also successful in reducing turnover.

The third group, with the work overload issue, went through the diagnostic process, which resulted in the identification of a need for restructuring so that work could be accomplished in more logical ways. The final recommendation was therefore to reorganise the department and this was also adopted. Although this paved the way for more flexible ways of working, the main recommendation did not focus on this.

The second pilot was less successful in bringing about change but did provide considerable opportunities for learning. It proved difficult to generate the participation and involvement of staff in the initial diagnostic stage. Recommendations were made but not implemented because the staff had not fully participated at the initial stage and subsequently rejected the outcomes.

There were a number of reasons for the lack of success in this business area. First, it was a much larger group than the others. There were approximately a hundred staff and this proved much more difficult than working with smaller teams. Second, morale was low and there was very low trust of management. Moreover, the company did have a preset agenda—confirming employee suspicions. Management wanted to use the process to introduce new working arrangements with shift patterns. They were not adopting a dual agenda and encouraging staff to come up with ideas, which would benefit all. This group therefore did not feel that they were collaborating but rather that a new way of working was being imposed on them in a devious way and they rejected this. They mistrusted management's motives and were not convinced it was the right thing to do.

The element of two-way trust, which is crucial to the change process, was therefore missing in this sector. Management were also very resistant and reluctant to experiment. Some small group work was carried out in this area and the project team felt that progress could have been made with some teams. However, management resisted this. They wanted flexibility to be all or nothing because they believed that, otherwise, it would fragment the business and be more difficult to manage. Managers did not feel able or want to manage the resistance and lack of trust among staff. In fact, this business area had other complications and it later closed down and the work was relocated elsewhere. HR was not in possession of all this information and, therefore, it was not possible to address these issues in the change process, which was therefore doomed to failure. This underlines the importance of looking at and understanding the total context.

Given the complexity of this pilot, the process was also limited by shortage of time and resources—only one HR manager was working on this project and he had limited time. He felt that, although HR had an important role to play in ensuring consistency of the process and providing tools and training, an external person or team with more time would have been better able to work with the deeper problems and identify and challenge counterproductive assumptions perpetuating inappropriate practices and culture in this case. Real and sustainable change takes time and resources, which are beneficial in the long term. But, in this case the goal was a "quick fix", neglecting the current situation.

This group would therefore have benefited from a more in-depth process in which time was taken to explore all aspects of their work, practices and context, challenge counterproductive assumptions and confront and work with, rather than ignore resistance, particularly among managers. A more explicit and highly developed dual agenda of enhancing workplace effectiveness and employee (including manager) benefit may also have been more successful in engaging the teams and stimulating innovation. If staff had been able to talk about their personal needs and had felt that these were taken into consideration, this would have been likely to release energy and motivation to change—and perhaps helped to overcome the suspicion of the company's motives.

Resistance

There was much initial scepticism and concerns from both staff and management in all the pilot groups and beyond throughout the organisation. Many staff thought that there was going to be a "catch", reflecting distrust of the company motives. They also feared that there was going to be an overall approach, which would not take account of the needs and circumstances of specific sections of the business. The response of HR was to state that recommendations would not be compulsory and people could choose not to adopt them. In fact, in situations where flexible working arrangements were introduced there was a minority of employees who took the option to stick to nine to five working with paid overtime. Most felt sufficiently involved in the decision-making process to go with the process from the outset, even if it meant loss of overtime earnings. Others did so at a later stage, challenging the assumption that most people would prefer to work longer hours and earn extra money than to have flexible working times.

There was also initial resistance from managers, many of whom perceived this as an HR rather than a business strategy and believed that it was going to be something extra to manage:

> ... the managers were very sceptical, they thought that it was an HR thing, that it couldn't possibly have any business benefit, and it's just hassle to manage. So, why would they want to do it? there was a lot of opposition, and quite a lot of negativity.

Resistance from managers mainly reflected concern about whether they would be able to manage flexible working arrangements, which they perceived as time-consuming. They anticipated that it was going to be difficult for them to monitor which employees should be working on any given day. The HR team dealt with this resistance by helping the managers to develop flexible working timetables. Those managers who were resistant could then see who should be working when and accepted this. This is one effective way of getting reluctant managers to accept change and to challenge the assumption that flexible working is difficult to manage. But, of course, it does not challenge beliefs in the importance of being able to see staff working to know that they are doing their jobs. Mutual trust takes longer to develop.

Low trust and the reluctance of many managers to trust their staff to work without face-to-face supervision underpins another stumbling block—most managers, even if they accept flexibility for their staff, are reluctant to work flexibly themselves. However, this is slowly beginning to change. Some managers now work at home on occasions and one of the pilot group managers also negotiated flexibly for herself of the pilot process.

After the pilots, other managers heard about the success of flexible working in two of the groups and approached the project team to ask if they could follow suit. In the end, the changes became demand-driven and the HR team was actually overwhelmed by the high volume of demand. Flexibility is spreading, but further initiatives will be needed to enhance mutual trust, which is so crucial for the success of this initiative.

DIFFUSION

When the pilots were completed the successes were communicated throughout the business. HR contacted each of the senior managers with a remit to talk to them about doing a similar thing. However, diffusion of the process did not work in this structured way. Rather, line managers and staff from the two successful pilots were ambassadors for the process. Other line managers began to contact HR asking for their departments to be involved in similar processes. Thus, diffusion became demand-driven. People could see the benefits and were keen to undergo a similar process and implement changes.

Some of the managers who had been most vocal against flexibility later adopted the process. However, they learned about the process and then led it themselves, rather than involving HR. This was useful because the business issues were clearly on the table. The HR champion of this process admits that:

> ... if its HR-led it's often regarded as fluffy, not business-driven.

Of course, the results of line-manager-led initiatives, like those of the pilot studies, vary. Now, HR is offering training in the process to line managers. Their goal is to get management engagement in and commitment to the process and to give them the tools to manage the process themselves.

SOME OUTCOMES

- Formal evaluation is in progress. At the time of writing, the company expects to complete the evaluation shortly and hopes to gain a clear picture of the benefits of flexible working. Currently, 50% of the workforce is working flexibly as a result of the diffusion process.

- The HR manager felt that this process and the outcomes have changed the whole culture and attitude to working patterns and practices from the grass roots level upwards and believes this is one of the most significant outcomes of the change process. Flexible working is now accepted as the norm, not the exception. The behaviour and culture of the company reflect this. Flexible working is now recognised as a benefit to the organisation as well as the staff.

- After the trial period, most of the people who had opted out wanted to work flexibly and were prepared to forgo overtime earnings.

- Team relations improved because there was no longer any backlash against mothers working flexibly—this was now a genuine option for all.

- Services for clients also improved, as there was no longer a need to rely on overtime goodwill.

- High staff turnover in some parts of the business has reduced and the flexibility that has been introduced has proved to be a selling point for recruitment and retention.

- Thus, the assumptions that most people would rather earn more money than have free time (and so would be reluctant to exchange paid overtime for more flexible working hours) and that managing flexible working will be time-consuming have both been challenged.

Moreover, enhanced client service has challenged the view that working hours in financial services must mirror those of their clients.

- Employees benefited in numerous ways from having more flexibility to integrate their work and non-work commitments. For example, an employee who had worked a three-day week went back to full-time work because she was able to have flexitime within that and be able to fit in other responsibilities. Men were particularly pleased with the changes because it had been more difficult for them than for women to negotiate informal flexibility.

Senior managers appeared to have been converted to the more flexible approaches to working patterns. A year after the changes were first introduced, managers were even suggesting that something was wrong in a department if it did not have any flexible working arrangements and negative comments about flexibility were rarely heard. This has come about over time as more work groups actually implement the process and see it work in practice.

However, the flexible working options developed in this process remain rather formal and prescribed. There remains some reluctance to view employees' needs for flexibility as an opportunity to innovate and to pursue a dual agenda in which flexible solutions are sought that give equal weight to the needs of the business and employees' quality of life. But, the process is ongoing and mutual trust, which is essential to mutual flexibility, always takes time to develop, particularly in an environment with traditionally low trust on all sides. Moreover, there are signs that some mutual trust is beginning to develop with some managers prepared to say that they do not mind when and where work is done, providing it is done well and on time, and staff recognising that there are no hidden agendas.

LESSONS LEARNED FROM THIS CASE STUDY

- Within one organisation, different business areas have different issues. These need to be addressed in the change process in order to achieve appropriate outcomes in a range of contexts.

- A focus on working practices rather than starting with the needs of certain sectors of the workforce, such as parents of young children, helps to bring about changes in the structure and culture of work.

- Flexibility is not just for women or parents of young children. Men particularly welcomed the new, inclusive, flexible forms of work because, while some women had been able to negotiate one-off flexible arrangements, men had not previously felt able to do so.

- An early diagnostic stage, where employees are engaged in thinking about actual work demands and practices and encouraged to question the way things have always been done, is an important stage in developing alternative ways of working based on the unique needs of specific work groups or departments.

- Employee participation and collaboration between staff, management and a change agent is crucial for staff to feel ownership of and therefore commitment to new ways of working.

- The change process is sometimes easier to achieve with smaller groups than a large group.

- Predetermined solutions to a prior agenda involve using the process as a way of getting people to accept changes and are not effective.

- For innovation to occur, it is necessary to be open to new ideas beyond standard forms of flexibility.

- It is necessary to be alert to other possible needs for optimising flexibility and staff well-being—which may precede flexibility—for example, reorganisation.

- The change process needs to be considered in context—treating flexibility as an add-on option without taking into account the full situation, including business intentions and staff morale will not be successful.

- An HR-led initiative will not always be taken seriously by line managers, who may regard the process as a "soft" initiative rather than a business one, though support from HR is crucial.

- It may be preferable for the process to be led by an external person who would not take working practices and culture for granted. Line managers, if well trained and resourced, can also lead the change process effectively.

- There was a view that more widespread change would have required additional resources in terms of HR staff time or an external facilitator. Quick-fix, under-resourced initiatives do not work.

- Developments are limited by a greater focus on business needs, rather than on a dual agenda in which business and employee needs are both considered equally, which can release greater creativity and innovation.

- Mutual trust is critical and success will always be limited in its absence.

- A focus on the visibility of staff and/or managers' own visibility at all times is a symptom of low trust and undermines innovation.

- Changes in the management style of resistant managers will require that they understand that flexibility will bring benefits to the organisation.

- Organisational learning is always uneven, with some managers and departments taking longer than others to develop mutual trust and commitment to mutually advantageous solutions.

- Piloting the change process, evaluating outcomes and assessing learning points—both positive and negative—are important for overcoming some of the resistance and for organisational learning.

- Successful change processes and initiatives can be communicated and diffused across the organisation. Those managers and members of staff who have been involved in pilot initiatives can be powerful ambassadors for change.

- Change is an ongoing process. The next stage at Adminco will be to continue to address the focus on input rather than output, mutual trust and innovation.

CHAPTER 8

Charityco

Reflections from a chief executive

BACKGROUND

Charityco is a charity and company limited by guarantee. It has been established for over 30 years and provides services for learning-disabled children and adults. At the start of the project Charityco had a staff team of approximately 50 (whole-time equivalent) providing 24-hour care 365 days a year.

As a social care provider, many of its outcomes are hard to measure, as they are subjective and related to qualitative issues in the delivery of care. Its "customers" are its residents and because of their severe disability they are unable to give Charityco formal feedback. Therefore, the company relies on others close to it or other agencies involved in the care of its customers to measure its success. One of the main factors that promotes good quality care is stability and quality of staff and this is essential for high-quality care because Charityco's residents rely on the staff team to meet all their daily needs.

The increasing pressures faced by the social care sector influenced the company's need and rationale for change. There have been many changes within the field over the last five years and the major impact for the company was that retention of staff had become a real concern. Changes in legislation meant that the recruitment and training requirements for all care staff have become very expensive, thus making improved retention imperative. Charityco had a reasonably low turnover of staff, but any improvement has a direct financial benefit to the organisation and, being a small charity, this can have a major impact. The other very important reason for retaining staff is the provision of consistency for Charityco's residents and this improves the quality of the care it provides.

Despite trying to attract more male staff, the majority of Charityco's staff were women (95%), most of whom had some degree of childcare responsibility; 70% of the staff were part time. The company also had problems retaining female staff after they went on maternity leave and some staff were under pressures trying to juggle childcare and family commitments.

Whilst there was a broad commitment to the project by all involved, the reality was that Charityco's understanding of the notion of work–life balance was mixed and overall fairly limited. Most of the team at Charityco had a preconceived idea that the integration of work and personal life would be very difficult to achieve in a social care environment. It appeared that many team members had assumed that it primarily applied to staff who had young children and had latched onto many of the concrete outcomes that might arise out of the project, such as job-sharing.

All these issues were magnified by the fact that the organisation had an ambitious business plan that set out a significant growth in business both in diversity and size over the next few years.

THE PROCESS

The trustees and senior management had always recognised the link between a happy, satisfied workforce and the delivery of care. They had demonstrated their commitment through achieving the Investors in People Award[1] in 1998 (the organisation was reaccredited in 2001). There had always been a willingness to respond to individual staff needs regarding shift patterns, but this was done on a rather *ad hoc* basis and therefore not very equitably. Job-sharing had also been agreed for certain individuals, but this was not set up as a formal arrangement and resulted merely in two part-time staff sharing a shift pattern.

Prior to the project all stakeholders were made aware, via all the company's usual communication systems, such as newsletters/team meetings/supervision, that Charityco was applying to the DTI (Department of Trade and Industry) for participation in the Challenge Fund[2] project. It also circulated various papers and press cuttings and, by doing so, hoped to start people thinking about what work–life balance could mean for them and the impact on Charityco. It also hoped to engender some enthusiasm.

Involvement in this project had been initiated by the CEO, but the trustees had been in full agreement; so, the initial meetings with consultants involved the trustees and the chief executive. For some of the trustees the notion of work–personal life balance or integration was a new concept and one that they could not imagine applying within their own professional world. The trustees worked in law, surveying, medicine and management and were largely men in their late 50s or early 60s; so, throughout their own careers they had been expected "to put in the hours", often at a cost to their own personal life. At this first meeting the consultants made a presentation and there was an opportunity for discussion and debate. Whilst there was broad agreement that this was "the right thing to do", it would also be fair to say that some of the trustees struggled to see the correlation between employee work–personal life integration and the effectiveness of Charityco. This was largely due to their own professional norms and the nature of Charityco's business. Regardless of this they gave their blessing and an undertaking to carry through any realistic recommendations that

[1] Investors in People is an organisation that provides criteria for best practice in human resource management. Public, private and charitable organisations can apply to be assessed and once completed successfully are awarded an Investors in People status.
[2] The UK Government's Department of Trade and Industry set up a Work–Life Balance Challenge Fund to provide financial support through consultancy to public, private and charitable organisations in its efforts to introduce more flexible working arrangements.

might be made. Senior staff were given an opportunity to meet the consultants on a one-to-one basis to discuss their own individual work–personal life integration needs, wants and desires and that of their team. The consultants then made themselves available to the wider staff team in one-to-one meetings. In addition to the meetings, all staff were canvassed through a questionnaire. In order to promote consultation, work–personal life issues were discussed within team meetings and fed back to the CEO.

What Was Discovered as Part of the Assessment Process?

Throughout the organisation there were preconceived ideas that work–personal life issues or "work–life balance" as it was known, really applied only to those with young children. The groups who inadvertently excluded themselves were older staff, ancillary staff and management. There was also a degree of cynicism that changes taking account of people's personal life wouldn't work in social care.

WHAT AREAS WERE FOCUSED ON?

1. That Work Life Issues Apply to All Sectors Including Social Care

There was a discussion on the use of self-rostering. This was considered as a very positive opportunity so that individuals and teams could take on some responsibility for their own working schedules. The issues involved were explored in a one-day workshop. The workshop was far too much of a challenge to supervisors who had already seen a significant amount of change since the appointment of the current CEO. There was a great deal of resistance and the supervisors chose to embrace the principals whilst maintaining control of the rotas them-selves. It was not possible to work with the supervisors' resistance at this stage; however, the process of exploring this option was positive in itself as it demonstrated a commitment to inclusive management styles.

2. It Is Relevant for Managers

At the start of the project the CEO struggled within her own role partly due to the pressures she faced as a working parent and partly due to issues relating to governance and decision making. As part of the project, consideration was given to her carrying out her role as a job share and also the option of part-time working. The project proved a catalyst for her as she (finally) recognised that work–personal life issues were as relevant for senior managers as any other team member. In fact, to some degree as a senior member of staff her attitude to work–personal life issues was more important because her ability to carry out her role had a potential to impact on everyone. In order to consider the CEO's role and how it might alter, all senior staff had a one-to-one meeting with consultants. From this all the necessary functions of the whole management team were spelled out and the positive areas and the areas of weakness were highlighted. It was very clear that the strategic areas required could easily be fit into three days, which was a very positive gain for the CEO but also enabled others to take on additional areas of responsibility. This gave the organisation a far stronger second tier of senior management and in addition provided team members with "development opportunities".

So, it was decided that the CEO would change her working pattern. The major challenge involved was the need for change in mindset for all involved. The CEO needed to make sure that she delegated the right tasks, to the right people within the right timescales, which wasn't always easy. Initially, she took a lot of work home which has been a hard habit to break. Prior to the project she assumed that she could do everything—hectic career, contributing family member and good citizen—but the project taught her that whilst she can do all these things she may need to consider to what extent and how effectively. The CEO now recognises that she can give her best to all these roles if she stands back and considers how much real time and energy she really has and wants to give to each role. She hopes that by demon-strating to others that she can make a worthy contribution without working 60 hours week that they will be gentler with themselves!

Over the last 18 months many people have said to the CEO: I wish I could reduce my hours/work in a different way/reduce my stress, etc. The CEO's response has been that work–personal life issues are something that we all need to take ownership of and, whilst we can't all achieve satisfactory integration of our roles all of the time, from small beginnings ...

3. Older Staff

As part of the project Charityco looked at phased retirement which enabled staff to reduce not only their hours but if mutually acceptable their responsibilities as they approached retirement age. For three senior staff this proved to be a really positive move. They took the opportunity to take up posts involving less supervision and reduce their hours for the organisation. Through this process staff were retained who had 43 years of service between them and they were on hand to share that wealth of knowledge and experience with new post holders. The company is optimistic that they will remain with the firm, working reduced hours, past their original retirement age, thus extending their valuable contribution to the organisation.

4. Focus on Recruitment and Retention

Reviewing the "real" cost of recruiting and retaining staff helped senior staff to focus their minds on the whole recruitment procedure. They introduced "taster shifts" as part of the recruitment and selection process. This gave both parties the chance to consider their decision further. Most people enjoy these shifts but some do not take up the post and are grateful to find out early on that it's not for them. This saves the organisation a great deal of resources inducting someone who doesn't stay. Senior staff also reviewed adverts/job descriptions and person specifications and have now attracted a wider cross section of staff offering more comprehensive and diverse care.

5. Maternity Returnees

Since the project all women who have had time off for maternity leave have returned to the company, which has been far more proactive before and during maternity absence. Charityco now tries to be as creative as practical and offer reduced or altered shift patterns that fit in with family life. This has meant that the company has retained over 27 years of experience in the last two years.

LEARNING POINTS

- At times it was difficult to maintain the momentum of the project because the CEO had taken on too much responsibility for it and not enabled others to have ownership.

- With hindsight the CEO says she would have recruited one change agent within each team to promote communication—not always the line manager.

- The CEO is honest with people and explains that it hasn't been easy and that it took a long time for her to stop apologising for the days she wasn't available, but it has been possible. The CEO says she was also very fortunate to have a board of trustees who had trust in her and a willingness to try this creative approach.

- One of the key messages the company had to get across was that, whilst the goal was focused on individuals, it still had to remain clear about the overall organisational aims. Individually and collectively staff had to meet these aims but also be mindful of the best outcomes for all staff members on the way.

LESSONS LEARNED FROM THIS CASE STUDY

- The organisation managed to retain many experienced and competent staff—all the women who have been on maternity leave have stayed with the organisation following their babies' arrivals. Some are on the same terms and conditions, others are working fewer hours.

- Five staff members have been attracted back to the organisation who had left for various reasons.

- Three staff chose to take on posts with less responsibility before retirement, whereas previously they would have left the organisation.

- All staff are aware that the company offers greater flexibility in work patterns, responsibility and career development.

- Greater staff retention and therefore continuity to the service that Charityco provides.

- As an organisation Charityco is less focused on attendance and now keen to explore the concept of working from home, job-sharing or part-time working.

- When people from within the organisation and external to it realise that someone with strategic responsibility can work part time and carry out their duties effectively and competently, whilst being a good family member and citizen, it does cause them to question their attitudes.

CHAPTER 9

A Long-term View

This book has aimed to explore ways in which organisations can address the challenges presented by changing internal and external contexts by implementing changes that enhance employees' opportunities to integrate their work and personal lives, and, in so doing, enhance workplace effectiveness in rapidly changing environments. We have tried to avoid presenting simplistic accounts that focus on outcomes and gloss over the glitches that inevitably occur. Rather, we have emphasised some of the problems and learning points encountered en route—some resolved, others still being worked upon. The organisations are at different stages in the learning process. Some have moved beyond the stage of adapting to the needs of individual employees to develop wider changes and are recognising the value of innovative working arrangements but have not yet reached the stage of two-way trust where they can let go of the need to formalise and constrain the use of non-standard ways of working. They are already gaining many benefits but are yet to reap the full potential advantages of the process of collaboratively questioning taken-for-granted assumptions and rethinking ways of working. Others have gone much further, achieving transformational learning— either organisation-wide (easier in smaller organisations) or in parts of organisations, with a need for more diffusion of experience. Here,

Box 9.1   A Role for Trade Unions

Trade Unions can help organisations to work towards win–win solutions. For example, the TUC (Trades Union Congress) in Britain has worked with a number of unions and employers' organisations to encourage innovations in public and private sector organisations. Their initiatives reflect the case studies in this book in that:

- There is a focus on *process* and not just outcomes.
- The process draws on *collaboration* and partnership between unions and management to find solutions to both organisational issues and employees' work–personal life needs.
- The process includes involving staff in decisions about change, making sure their personal needs and aspirations as well as organisations' concerns are considered (*a dual agenda*).
- Recognises the crucial need for *commitment from the top*.
- *Pilot projects* are used to try out new ways of working in "safe" contexts.

Bristol City Council

The TUC worked with the Employers' Organisation for Local Government, Bristol City Council and council trade unions—GMB, TGWU and Unison—on a project sponsored by the European Union to explore potential innovative working patterns that would improve both the quality of the Council's services and employees' lives.

Initial research using surveys and focus groups showed that although people wanted more time for family, education or other activities, the most common reason for wanting change was the desire to work more effectively in an uninterrupted and focused way. As an example, a pilot flexible working project was set up in Library Services where staff had low morale following recent cuts in the staffing budget and were wary of the idea of Sunday opening which had been suggested in a recent customer survey. Staff were asked who would like to work on Sundays (for additional payments), although no one was compelled to do so. Additional members of staff were then recruited to work alongside the regular staff who had volunteered to work on Sundays—many of whom were part-timers keen to increase their hours. A further staff initiative was self-rostering, where staff organised shifts on a team basis so that they felt in control of their time and organised work more effectively. The outcomes were an enhanced local service by the provision of Sunday opening, increased use of libraries, especially by families, and more flexibility of working time for staff.

For more details of this and other initiatives by the TUC see *www.tuc.org.uk/ changing times/casestudies*

work-personal life issues are regarded as an opportunity to experiment with different ways of working. Systemic change involving shifts in working practices, structures and cultures takes time and effort and progress tends to be uneven across different units within large organisations. But, the outcomes can be very positive. Unlike short-term quick fixes, such as the development of policies without changes to the system in which they operate, this approach has long-term pay-offs. Change is ongoing and unremitting in the current global context and this approach offers a process which can be used to deal with new issues as they arise, rather than having to go back to the drawing board to address each new situation. There will never be a final solution unless external and internal contexts stop changing, which is unlikely. Thus, an understanding of the process of change and the importance of the dual agenda together with sensitivity to new and emerging issues can help organisations to maximise their human resources. But, is this enough in the long term?

In the case studies we have emphasised the dual agenda of workplace effectiveness and personal quality of life. The business case for change is important, but for initiatives to be sustainable employees' needs should also be kept on the agenda. Employee commitment to and feelings of ownership of new ways of working are necessary if changes are to be successful. Equally, a process that considers only the personal outcomes for employees and not the benefits to the organisation will be doomed to failure. This is a dual agenda, but we may also need to think, in the long term, of a multiple agenda which incorporates wider societal changes. This involves looking beyond short-term business arguments to consider the long-term impact of current ways of working. In the context of the global economy, work is becoming more demanding and intensified everywhere, in private and public sectors, as more work is undertaken by fewer people (Peper, Lewis & Den Dulk, 2004). Innovative flexible working arrangements can help, but we need to recognise that these too can create problems in some cases. We have seen (e.g., in the case of

Energyco) that there is a danger that high levels of autonomy can create blurred boundaries between work and home, in which case people often "choose" to work longer and harder to fulfil all their demands (Lewis, 2003b). This tends to be exacerbated if jobs are perceived as insecure. In addition, although we have seen in this book that innovations, such as self-managed teams, can be highly successful in meeting business and personal needs, this too has to be monitored. Research in organisations across Europe indicate that, although this type of innovation can work very well, devolving responsibility for flexibility from managers to colleagues and building solidarity among teams, this solidarity does have limits and can create new tensions even among the most cohesive of teams (Peper et al., 2004). Thus, new solutions—such as flexibility and autonomy with high trust, or self-rostering and self-managing teams— can paradoxically also lead to new issues and have the potential for creating new problems.

Thinking long term, these problems could affect the sustainability of human resources and organisational effectiveness (Lewis & Cooper, 1999). But, it does not end there. If current trends of long hours and intensification continue, we also need to think about the social consequences of working practices which undermine work–personal life integration, for families, communities and wider societies (see Lewis, Rapoport et al., 2003). Stress and burnout are just some of the outcomes that can threaten individuals, families and organisations. Another consequence of intense workloads, for example, is the decline in the birth rate in many countries, as couples are unable to manage two demanding occupational roles and consider having children. This is a major concern in many countries, especially Italy and Japan, where there is a fear that in the longer term there will be a dire shortage of workers and consumers. Thinking long term then requires employers to consider individual and social consequences of working practices as well short-term economic outcomes.

At the European level, a public policy approach to the organisation of work is being advocated which centres on achieving improved social sustainability of working life (Webster, 2004). The aim is to bring about changes in Europe's workplaces, to create the conditions in which work and life are mutually enhancing rather than being mutually diminishing. This suggests that long-term thinking in workplaces needs to focus on achieving both financial and social sustainability of work and organisations. Juliet Webster (2004, p. 9) argues that:

> ... *improving and sustaining the competitiveness of national economies and companies is an important objective, and policy discussions connect economic competitiveness with quality of working life and quality of life more broadly. Economic performance, in this discourse, has to be balanced with socially sustainable forms of work organisation, with quality jobs, and with the maintenance and improvement of the quality of life in its broadest sense. ... In EU social and employment policy, there is a belief that these various objectives are not only compatible and mutually achievable, but also that they are mutually supporting and complementary.*

This is the approach that is advocated in this book and the case studies demonstrate that a dual agenda approach can be very effective in bringing about transformation to meet the changing environment. Some of the key principles for bringing about sustainable change to meet the dual agenda of workplace effectiveness and employee opportunities for work–personal life integration that have emerged in this book, albeit not all used in every case, include:

• Working collaboratively with work teams.

• Examining assumptions that underpin work practices undermining the dual agenda.

• Keeping the dual agenda in sight at all times.

• Collaborating at every stage.

• Working with resistance as a positive force, and using action research to pilot new, collaboratively designed interventions in a non-judgemental context.

But, is it enough to focus just on workplace level change, and can the change process discussed in these case studies and the principles on which it is based be applied more widely? We suggest that, although it is beyond the scope of this book to explore in more detail, a long-term approach to organisational success needs to be contextualised within a

Box 9.2   Sickness Absence as a Work–Personal Life Issue

Eurobank is a major European bank which initiated a culture change programme to address problems of high rates of sick leave, stress and recruitment difficulties. These were believed to be related to work–personal life
issues but work–life policies were having no effect because of low take-up in
a dominant traditional culture which idealised employees as being available
at all times.

The company undertook one of a series of experiments, initially partially
funded by the Dutch Government as part of their programme on Daily
Routine Incentive Schemes, to stimulate new arrangements for a better
balance between work and care. The first year of the experiment was so
successful that the company then funded the project for a further two years.

External consultants/researchers used an approach that they termed Theme
Centred Interaction (TCI) (see van den Bogaard, Callens & Van Iren, 2003 for
more details). This is a process-driven approach, building on some aspects of
the work of Rapoport, Bailyn, Fletcher and Pruitt (2002) and also psycho-
analyst Ruth Cohn (Cohn, 1983). This model focuses on the quality of
interactions between individuals, in the context of a changing environment,
to generate learning and transformation capabilities in groups of people
within organisations.

Although relatively unique, this approach reflects the aspects of change
processes in this book in that:

- It starts from a belief that occupational and personal priorities need not
  be in conflict but can enhance each other—the dual agenda.
- It involves using a work–personal life lens to study the way work is
  performed, reveal norms, values and organisational structures, legitimise
  open discussion of personal as well as business priorities, identify
  inefficient practices that employees report they experience as hamper-
  ing performance and making the integration of work and personal life
  difficult, seeking new win–win solutions and implementing experiments
  for change.
- This process was initially carried out within pilot projects focusing on
  specific areas of the bank.
- Support was available from senior management, which is regarded as
  crucial.

- Working with resistance is regarded as crucial.

- Learning is diffused more widely through the training of (internal) facilitators.

Sickness Absence

High rates of sickness absence emerged from conversations and interviews as a major issue for managers and also co-workers who have to cover for absent colleagues. Much of the illness was related to work in some way (e.g., stress from poor relationships at work), but managers were resistant to the idea that they might play a role in this, assuming that sick leave was a purely private matter or an issue for the welfare department.

Interventions developed collaboratively included more guidance for co-workers on covering for sickness absence. Also, managers began to interview the long-term sick at home and encourage them to come into work to talk with managers and colleagues. Often work-related problems related to specific interactions were identified and could then be worked with to change the situations.

Outcomes of these interventions included enhanced employee productivity and performance and a dramatic decline in sickness absence from 14.6% to 1.6% over the first year.

multiple agenda; that is, we need to ask: How can we ensure that future developments benefit organisations, employees and also families, communities and the wider society in which organisations operate? How can work and workplaces be socially as well as economically sustainable in the long term?

Based on a study of work–personal life integration in seven countries[1] (UK, USA, India, South Africa, Japan, Norway and The Netherlands), Lewis, Rapoport et al. (2003) argue that these societies seem stuck about how to make equitable, satisfying and sustainable changes in the ways in which paid work can be combined with the rest of life and they emphasise the need to rethink and question many deeply held—but outdated—

[1] The study *Work–Personal Life Integration: Looking Backwards to Go Forwards in Seven Countries* was funded by the Ford Foundation by a grant to the Institute of Family and Environment Research, see Footnote 1 in Chapter 1.

assumptions about working practices, families, culture and personal lives:

> *In this (contemporary) context we argue that there is now a need to think creatively about how to implement new ways of equitably distributing paid work and integrating this with the rest of life in ways that enhance people's life satisfaction, productivity and potential. Work–personal life integration issues need to form an integral part of discussions around the "new, global economy".*

Lewis, Rapoport and Gambles (2003, p. 4)

At the end of this study a scenario-planning meeting was held bringing together creative thinkers from each country (from business, unions, academia and the media) to consider visions for the future and practical ways of moving forward these issues. The report of this meeting is contained in Appendix B. It is hoped that this will provoke some thoughts among those interested in long term sustainability of business and societies about these larger issues.

Work–Life Integration Change Process

INTERVIEW SCHEDULE

Introduction

Please describe the nature of your business/company—to help set the context for the interview.

The Work–Life Change Process

Before

- Tell me about the work–life change process that has been introduced to your company.

- Why did you want to change? What were the problems you were addressing?

- What steps had you already taken before the changes began?

During

- Who was involved in the change process? Was there any collaboration? If so, with whom? With the workforce? Work groups? What were the consequences?

- What steps did the process involve?

- What were the problems at each stage? What were the learning points?

- Did you encounter any resistance? If so, from whom? Why? What were the assumptions underpinning resistances in your opinion?

- How did you engage with resistance? What were the successes and the learning points?

After

- What were the outcomes of the change process?

- Have you evaluated the process and the changes? What were the learning points?

- How might you have done things differently with hindsight?

- Is there any other advice you would give to someone starting on this process?

Work–Personal Life Harmonisation: Visions and Pragmatic Strategies for Change

Summary of reflections arising from a scenario meeting,
23–24 March 2004

Rhona Rapoport, Suzan Lewis and Richenda Gambles

The harmonisation of paid work with other parts of people's lives is a central issue for many societies and people today. As more and more people work longer or more intensely—be it because of perceived or absolute economic necessity, a response to societal or workplace expectations, or because they enjoy and derive fulfilment from paid work—key questions are emerging:

- What does such a lop-sided distribution between paid work and other parts of life do to people and societies in terms of equity or well-being?

- How does a lop-sided distribution between paid work and other parts of life impact on the sustainability of people, families and communities in terms of both changing demographics or a sense of dignity they are able to experience?

- What are current working patterns and expectations doing to time and energy available for family responsibilities, care and connectedness with others, leisure, and time to simply think, rest and refresh the spirit?

● And what opportunities are available for people who have other commitments or wish to dedicate time and energy to other non-paid parts of life?

These questions link with many issues connected to the global economic context in which our lives are unfolding. In research exploring work–personal life harmonisation[1] in India, Japan, The Netherlands, Norway, South Africa, the UK and the US, we have heard:

There used to be an imbalance towards the life side ... the change has been positive from the consumer point of view ... but there has been a reverse with an imbalance towards the work side. I feel kind of alienated ... from the family and community and maybe that, too, is why I have begun to concentrate on work so much.

(Indian woman)

People increasingly form relationships through the Internet because they have no time—they are always working.

(Japanese man)

Society is changing, but the way we think about working life hasn't. Everyone knows the present organisation of work does not work, but nobody is ready to translate this into actual practice, despite this having serious implications for gender equality and life satisfaction.

(Dutch man)

I think people are more disconnected because they are just too busy. I hear everyone say that there is not enough time to meet friends, to be with our families.

(Norwegian woman)

[1] With a grant to the Institute of Family and Environmental Research from the Ford Foundation, Rhona Rapoport, Suzan Lewis and Richenda Gambles have been engaged in an international project *Work–Personal Life Integration: Looking Backwards to Go Forwards*. This project focuses on thinking about what has happened over the past 40–50 years in seven countries with the hope of learning something from developments in the past about how to proceed in the future.

I do have friends, but hardly see them. I am in the office at weekends. That is my life. I don't want to work so hard, but I have found my work environment is my second home, even Sundays. I haven't been to church this year.

(South African woman)

I see distributed work, distributed friendships, basically an increasingly atomized world, and I think people are all feeling increasingly lonely.

(British man)

There are two trends in response to the current situation of long hours and workplace intensity: a return to traditional gender roles in families, or having no children. It is not that people are actively choosing these options, they just don't have other options at the moment.

(American man)

These quotes illustrate some of the current discontents people from around the world voice about harmonising the many parts of their lives: discontents connected to a current lop-sided distribution of time and energy given to paid work. These discontents are exacerbated because work–personal life harmonisation connects with a number of other issues felt across a range of countries. Experiences of harmonising paid work with the rest of life are both affected by and affect falling birth rates; the emergence of stress-related sickness and also epidemics, such as HIV/AIDS; changing needs and wishes of men and women and relationships between them; changing family structures and values; changing practices and valuing of paid work; and the current global economy that brings affluence to some, poverty to many and tends to encourage long and intensive working practices.

Work–personal life harmonisation issues are experienced in the context of diverse cultural expectations, levels of government, workplace, family and personal life support (or lack of it), and varying economic and social contexts and conditions But, many of the core issues are similar, across the different contexts, particularly as globalisation and technology have made the world more interdependent. For many people, the push for ever more "efficient" (in the sense of less expensive) but not necessarily effective ways of working has led to increasingly long and/or intensive working hours and more intensive lives. Issues relating to the harmonisation of paid work with personal and family lives are central. They cannot be considered as purely personal, or as just family, employer or even national concerns. They are crucial issues of concern in the unfolding global economy.

WHERE ARE COUNTRIES NOW?

In order to optimise the experiences of people and societies in relation to work–personal life harmonisation, it is essential to understand where countries currently are in their evolutions of understanding and support for these issues. Here, we summarise briefly "where different countries are now" in relation to work–personal life harmonisation based on our research findings.

India

- Growing numbers of women in formal work in recent decades have posed challenges for ways in which paid work is harmonised with other parts of life, such as care responsibilities.

- Few legislative or welfare measures exist to help men and women harmonise paid work with personal lives.

- The opening of the economy has led to the importation of outsourced work and has increased the intensity and pressures of paid work for many people.

- Traditional extended families, which have previously offered so much work–personal life harmonisation support, are giving way to nuclear families in some areas and being challenged in others. This contributes to general life intensity.

- Concerns about work–life balance have emerged in this context, but workplace responses tend to be based on a US model of initiatives to support people to be able to work more rather than less.

- Work–life balance is seen as a luxury issue for a tiny majority and economic development is perceived as more urgent than "social well-being" and "people" issues.

Japan

- A low birth rate and ageing population partly reflect reactions to and causes of work–personal life harmonisation discontents. These have led to public policies for care leaves.

- But, gendered caring assumptions and high gender earning gaps remain: this perpetuates many inequities.

- Working environments are also very intensive, which poses work–personal life harmonisation issues for men as well as women.

- In this context, stress, rising divorce rate and relationship difficulties are occurring (as they are in many other countries).

- There are drives for "family-friendly" policies, but implementation gaps persist: change has not been systemic.

- Debates are emerging about how to change men's behaviour and workplace culture and practices, which highlight recognition that change so far has been insufficient.

- We hear of emerging hope and optimism for change in relation to work–personal life harmonisation—linked with responses to low birth rates and economic stagnation.

- Some unions are pushing for more rights for time out of work than wage increases, and advertisements are emerging that emphasise a more domestic male role.

The Netherlands

- Although this has traditionally been a single breadwinner society, a one-and-a-half earner "norm" has emerged creating new issues for work–personal life harmonisation.

- But, although gender inequities remain, there is limited concern about under-representation of women in top jobs.

- We hear many women "prefer" current part-time working patterns but would like men to work less as a strategy for easing work–personal life harmonisation.

- Some people also speak of the emergence of progressive forms of "feminine" leadership (as in other countries). These are regarded as softer and more collaborative management techniques, which, it is felt, may alter the ways that people are able to combine paid work with personal life.

- Progressive legislation also supports shared parenting as a way of easing work–personal life and gender equity concerns. Innovative government initiatives to stimulate change in organisations and society are emerging.

- But, global pressures often undermine such initiatives because of perceptions that competitiveness rests on "commitment" through long hours in some contexts, and the general intensification of work.

- In this context, burnout, sickness and disability leave, and early retirement issues are emerging, highlighting the problems that a lopsided focus on paid work can have on people, workplaces and society.

Norway

- High female labour market participation, supported by state policies including the "daddy month" leave, reflects attention to work–personal life harmonisation issues.

- A "state feminism" approach characterises much of the initiatives concerned with gender equity and work–personal life harmonisation. But, we hear that emerging shifts in emphasis to enable women to care at home are seen as moving back from this position.

- Despite all the support for work–personal life harmonisation, men and women report feeling pressurised to "have and do it all" in paid work and family life.

- In this context there is rising disability, stress and divorce, as in many other countries.

- Despite all the legislative support, there currently appears to be a lack of systemic and cultural change in workplace environments in relation to work–personal life harmonisation.

- We hear that globalisation "productivity" pressures undermine progressive policies and a focus on equity.

- Some people think gender equity, which is so connected with work–personal life harmonisation, is not increasing. But, others feel Norway is entering a new phase of development in relation to gender-equity issues.

South Africa

- The new "post-apartheid" constitution emphasises equality. But, compared with race, we hear there is less focus on gender-equity issues.

- There is no national debate on work–personal life harmonisation, but individual awareness of the issues is emerging as are organisational initiatives in some contexts to deal with this.

- A legacy of truth and reconciliation, in the context of race equality, highlights awareness about the importance of processes, rather than a quick fix, in enacting change.

- But, in the context of gender, we also hear that current approaches focus on increasing numbers of women in paid work rather than changing society to fit changing work–personal life harmonisation needs.

- We also hear that, at the moment, work–personal life harmonisation and gender issues are overshadowed by other concerns: AIDS, unemployment, crime, poverty.

- There is a backlash among some employers and groups of people to equity considerations and affirmative action promoting blacks and women in the workplace that can be constructed as threatening "efficiency".

- In this context, we hear of a "brain drain" as people leave the country in search of "better" opportunities.

- However, we hear that people are beginning to make some connections between work–personal life harmonisation and many of these issues.

The UK

- Although the growth of women in the labour market in the past half-century has been associated with developments of family-friendly or work–life balance initiatives, they still largely focus on individual solutions rather than systemic change. Initiatives also tend to be geared towards mothers, even though fathers need these initiatives too.

- There has been minimal compliance with EU directives relating to the reconciliation of paid employment with family life, although the government has recently encouraged voluntary actions by employers by promoting a business case for change. Nevertheless, long working hours and intensification of work remain and seem to be getting more acute.

- We hear of global "productivity" pressures, which also affect the extent to which policies for more optimal work–personal life harmonisations are introduced or implemented (as in many countries).

- We also find that flexible working arrangements are often associated with more work not less work (as in many other countries).

- For all the current hype about work–life balance, there is a feeling that the debate is feminised and stuck.

- Nevertheless we see some recent movement: government and pressure groups are raising issues of shared parenting; the provision of care by men as well as women; and the government is beginning to see this as a key issue relating to social justice.

The US

- Because of minimal state support, corporate-led work–life initiatives have emerged to ease the harmonisation of paid work and personal lives as more women have entered the formal paid labour market.

- But, as in other countries, these initiatives are often designed to enable men and women to work more rather than less.

- A work–life practitioner profession has emerged but tends to focus on HR organisational policies and initiatives, rather than viewing these as strategic issues more generally. Thus, work–personal life harmonisation tends to be marginalised as an issue, as are people making use of any such supports (as in other countries).

- In this context, policies for leave and diverse working practices are often undermined by intensive working conditions and cultures.

- Pockets of innovative research, exploring new ways that work could get done to be more equitable and efficient, are emerging (as they are in other countries, such as the UK and The Netherlands). But, despite these initiatives and the evidence produced advocating a synergy approach to work–personal life harmonisation, profits are generally considered more important than people.

- Many people say progress feels stuck: in fact, we hear there is uncertainty about what progress there is in the context of work–personal life harmonisation.

These brief overviews highlight that there have been country-specific impetuses for change in relation to work–personal life harmonisation issues. Norway, for example, has been prompted primarily by gender-equity concerns; and, in recent years, The Netherlands have been prompted by concerns relating to rising workplace stress and costly stress-related sickness leave. The UK situation has been influenced of late by EU directive requirements as well as awareness of the business case for change so as to maximise productivity; and concern over work–personal life harmonisation issues have largely been prompted by falling fertility rates in Japan. In the US the impetus for change in organisations has been centred on business needs and the need to recruit and retain skilled diverse workers, particularly women, although there is also mounting concern about families (including fathers) among pressure groups and researchers. In India change seems to be more connected with urbanisation and globalisation trends and economic development. And in South Africa we see economic development and business motivations to tackle the "brain drain", as the rationale for addressing work–personal life harmonisation issues, although HIV/AIDS has prompted growing concern over new ways to combine paid work with other needs and care activities.

But, regardless of prime motivations within these societies or levels or types of support made available, our country snapshots highlight that work–personal life harmonisation issues are being felt within all these different contexts. People within all these countries are experiencing work–personal life harmonisation discontents, which have been exacerbated by the global competitive economy. While the global economy is not new, the levels of exposure, mobility of people, money and businesses and the extent to which there is competition within and between countries mark relatively new developments. In this context many people, many workplaces and societies more generally seem to feel powerless to make changes that either introduce or develop initiatives to ease the harmonisation of paid work and personal life.

While the routes into looking at these issues are diverse, it seems that core underlying and unresolved tensions are similar in many contexts. No welfare state or society has managed to fully value the unpaid work done in families, primarily by women. Nor has any welfare state or society fully recognised the ways in which diverse personal life experiences and obligations feed into and affect experiences of paid work. These dilemmas are exacerbated by the competitive global economy. The global economic climate perpetuates and exacerbates notions of efficiency that involve fewer people doing more work as well as myths and assumptions that characterise "ideal workers" as those who can work as though they have few or no responsibilities outside of paid work.

In Norway, for example, there is extensive government support and collective ideological commitment to equity between men and women and equality more generally, which seems to help the harmonisation of paid work with personal life. But, because of growing competitiveness within workplace environments, people—particularly men—find it difficult to negotiate alternative working arrangements, downshift or take leaves that are formally available. In other countries, such as India or South Africa, there is a feeling that, despite some concern about work–personal life issues, it is not possible to implement any radical policies. The need for economic development to deal with many other concerns including widespread poverty is seen as much more pressing and at odds with work–personal life harmonisation strategies. There is a feeling in India and South Africa that "there is no alternative" to long or intensive working hours if they are to compete or "develop", despite the implications such an approach has for equity or well-being. In other countries, such as Japan or the US, which have a history of intensive workplace environments, while discontents are also emerging in relation to work–personal life harmonisation, few people feel able to challenge the status quo. They too see "no alternative". Many people fear jeopardising levels of income or already precarious levels of job security. We also see in countries, such as the UK or The Netherlands, that competition is affecting increasing numbers of people regardless of the sector or level in which they work. For example, the contracting out of many lower skilled jobs to agencies or cheaper country locations means more and more people are exposed to competitive or globalising forces. These trends and forces affect all the countries in our study. For example, we see this in the UK, which outsources much lower skilled work to cheaper countries, and in India, which receives some of this work. Competitive pressures around the world mean many people across countries feel unable to push for workplace change towards more optimal harmonisation of paid work and personal life. And this, despite the growing need as workforces become more diverse with varying personal life needs or responsibilities, and despite the potential benefits a more harmonised approach could bring for people and workplace effectiveness.

All in all, we hear that people in paid work around the world are working longer or more intensive hours. More seems to be expected of people in their paid work: physically, mentally and emotionally. This has implications for those in work, as well as for those who are unable to participate in paid work as fully as they might like because of a generic lack of consideration within workplaces of people's diverse personal life needs and situations. In this context, stress-related sicknesses and discontents are emerging within many countries.

These developments have implications for equity, well-being and sustainability in relation to work–personal life harmonisation issues within all these countries.

FUTURE THINKING: THE SCENARIO MEETING

In the final stage of our research (see Footnote 1 in Chapter 1) we brought together creative people[2] from the seven different participating countries in a small international meeting using scenario techniques. The aim of this meeting was to begin a "global" dialogue on the future of work–personal life harmonisation by making the time and space to think collaboratively about optimal harmonisations and strategies for moving forward. Participants discussed the directions in which societies were heading more generically, before envisioning the future of work–personal life harmonisation and collaborating on prag-

---

[2] This meeting, at Cumberland Lodge, Windsor, UK, on 23–24 March 2004, brought together *Lotte Bailyn* (USA), Professor of Management, MIT; *Pierre Brouard* (South Africa), Deputy Director, Centre for the study of AIDS; *Richenda Gambles* (UK), Research Associate, Institute of Family and Environmental Research; *Ian Greenaway* (UK), Managing Director, MTM; *Lisa Harker* (UK), Chair of Daycare Trust, freelance policy advisor and researcher; *Annemarie van Iren* (The Netherlands), freelance Management Consultant; *Sumiko Iwao* (Japan), Chair of the Gender Equality Council in the Prime Minister's Office; *Alex Jones* (UK), Senior Researcher, The Work Foundation; *Suzan Lewis* (UK), Professor of Organisational and Work–Life Psychology, Manchester Metropolitan University; *Jo Morris* (UK), Senior Policy Officer, Trades Union Congress; *Bram Peper* (The Netherlands), Postdoctoral Researcher, Erasmus University; *Rhona Rapoport* (UK), Director, Institute of Family and Environmental Research; *Vineet Sharma* (India), Chief Quality Officer, *Hindustan Times*; *Ragnhild Sohlberg* (Norway), Vice President, Hydro, Corporate Centre and Scientific Secretary, The European Research Advisory Board (EURAB); *Atle Taerum* (Norway), Agri Business Consultant/ Farmer; and *Kaiser Thibedi* (South Africa), Gender Trainer and Business Consultant.

matic strategies for change. There was a particular focus on moving the debate forward and the question of how to contribute to the development of work that is socially as well as economically sustainable.

Group discussions on where societies are currently situated in relation to work–personal life harmonisation and the critical points identified above led to the following observations:

1. Current forms of the globally competitive economy have led to intensified consumerism resulting in rising greed in terms of status, material possessions, wanting it all in all aspects of life and rising individualism. Gender identities and family structures have changed, which, while having the potential to be positive, presently tend to reflect or contribute to a devaluing of care. The effect of all of this is a decline in overall "wealth", if defined in a broader way, which incorporates human and social capital, and general well-being.

2. The negative aspects of Western consumer economies tend to erode communities, social values and attitudes, which, in turn, further fuels consumer economies. Legislation is being developed in some countries around working time limits, for example, to deal with and try to rectify negative implications of consumer economies and associated social erosions. But, legislation though necessary is not sufficient. The rise of new forms of globalisation and technology act as a super-boost to work–personal life harmonisation tensions, so legislation is insufficient in a global world. Does the current global economy sow the seeds of its own destruction, through forces such as demographic change? It seems the present global economy encourages people to live their lives in ways that may be unsustainable. But, it may also eventually provide the social forces necessary to facilitate change.

3. Current forms of capitalism, greed, money, consumerism and a tendency to place profits above people are driving current trends in each country and the directions that they are likely to take in the future in terms of work–personal life harmonisation, unless there is a fundamental shift in thinking. Global competition, efficiency drives and developments in information and communications technology often result in greater workplace intensity or longer hours

and the well-being of people is increasingly threatened.[3] Many societies seem to be moving from control (by norms and institutions) towards greater freedom, with increasing diversity of value systems and potential ways of living. The positive side of this shift towards freedom could be greater equity, balance and a sense of belonging. But, the negative aspects could be increasing greed, individualism, consumerism and inequities.

FUTURE THINKING: CRITICAL POINTS HOLDING BACK OPTIMAL CHANGE

Based on research prior to the international meeting, five critical points holding back optimal change in support of the harmonisation of paid work and the rest of life were identified. These were discussed and widely agreed upon by international participants. These critical barriers include:

- Limited thinking about alternatives to current implementations of market economies that also value people.

- Limited thinking about changing men–women relationships at all levels of society.

- Limited thinking about valuing those who "want a life" outside the workplace.

- Limited thinking beyond quick fixes.

- Limited thinking about the actual processes of change.

FUTURE THINKING: THE PROCESSES OF CHANGE

To move beyond these critical points it is important to understand and learn from cross-cultural comparisons of experiences of levers and

[3] Organisational case studies being carried out in private and public sector organisations in seven European countries, including two former communist regimes, indicate that the experience of intensification of work is widespread at diverse occupational levels. See *www.workliferesearch.org/transitions*

barriers to change, and to do so in a historical context. While experiences are by no means universal, generic levers for or drivers of change have emerged and continue to emerge at various times with varying impacts in different countries. These include:

- An influx of women into paid work.

- Changing men–women relationships.

- Changing family structures and values.

- Equality, equity and diversity drives.

- Recruitment and retention needs of employers.

- Demographic shifts including low birth rates and ageing populations.

- Advances in technology and blurring of boundaries between paid work and personal life.

- Increasing globalisation and changes in its characteristics.

- Emerging disease, disability, sickness and stress issues.

The influx of women from all walks of life into formal paid work has created ongoing challenges for individuals, families, workplaces and wider society about how to handle the distribution of paid work and non-paid caring responsibilities. Together with changing and diversifying family structures, this has altered gender roles, identities and relationships between women and men. Workplaces have sought in part to deal with some of these changes, for recruitment and retention reasons, or in some countries or contexts, because of equality, equity or diversity concerns. Changing relationships between women and men has the potential to lead to greater equity between men and women and enhanced life satisfaction if people are able to organise their lives in ways that enable a variety of aspects of life to be combined within their daily experiences. Moreover, technology can facilitate new and innovative ways of working that enable greater work–personal life integrations and harmonisation. All of this offers impetus for change.

There are diverse individual and societal responses to these various levers for change. There are pockets of innovation and optimism in some segments of societies. Some feel societies and people have entered a new phase in the evolution of these issues, in which the consequences of current and emerging working practices on people's lives—in all their diversity—are only just beginning to surface and be worked through. But, at the same time, many feel increasingly helpless and many people and societies appear stuck in thinking about how to move forward.

Building on the five critical points already highlighted, many ongoing or emerging barriers to change were identified in our international research and the scenario meeting. These include:

- Taboos and fears.

- Conflicts.

- Resistance.

- Growing individualism.

- Powerlessness.

- Limited connected thinking.

These barriers play out at many different levels of societies. For example, men's and women's fears and resistances about changing gender roles, identities and relationships with each other persist. Feelings of powerlessness against the supremacy of money and consumer forces are also apparent, as are taboos in relation to challenging the place and value of paid work in people's lives and within societies. It feels difficult—and many feel helpless—to challenge the current global economic framework that underpins contemporary values and practices. There is a widespread view, evident at the scenario meeting, in some sections of the media and our discussions with people in our international research that governments and different organisations within countries often focus on their own interests, without considering others: that there is less of a focus on collaborating with other countries, governments and organisations in ways that could enhance the well-being of others.

At the moment, there is too little connected thinking about how issues of work–personal life harmonisation affect and feed into many other social problems. Work–personal life harmonisation is a central issue facing societies today, which links with equity, well-being and sustainability issues across a range of experiences and "social problems". *It is vital to consider the ways in which work–personal life harmonisation issues are connected with many other problems or social forces in play today. But, this wider thinking can mean people feel unable to make concrete change. It is also crucial to act locally in ways that account for and incorporate bigger thinking. In other words, it is vital to see localised actions within a wider context.*

THE FUTURE: VISIONS

The societal and economic changes that occur over time are not linear. They are complex and can shift in various and sometimes unexpected ways. So, how will these situations develop? As we have stressed, work–personal life harmonisation links in with many other issues: of identity; of equity; of life satisfaction; of connectedness with others; of the provision and receiving of care; of changing gender roles and relationships between men and women. And all in the global economic context in which people's lives are unfolding. Discussions of many of these issues during the international meeting led to the development of a *scenario pathway framework* (see Figure B.1). This framework maps the pathways in which individuals and societies could develop in relation to work–personal life harmonisation.

During the meeting, dimensions of constraint, freedom, fragmentation and harmonisation were useful ways to capture something of the directions in which work–personal life harmonisation issues have and could continue to evolve. Using these dimensions, four possible directions for the future were identified. The top left-hand corner, which features the idea of "constrained harmonisations", reflects the pre-industrial past (but also reflects some societies or segments of societies today). This refers to a seamless yet largely unconscious and involuntary harmonisation of work and personal life, with little personal freedom. For example, men and women in agrarian economies often worked (or work) alongside each other in the many productive and reproductive

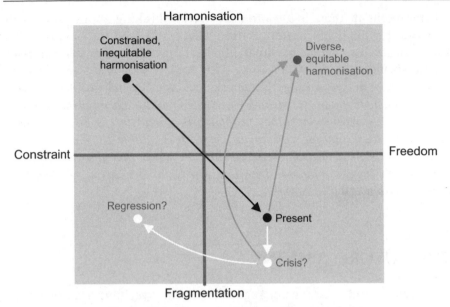

Figure B.1. Scenario pathway framework.

tasks, responsibilities or other parts of their lives. But, this was usually experienced in a patriarchal and inequitable context in which equity and well-being issues were not so widely considered. This has changed in many societies through the process of industrialisation with many people experiencing greater personal freedom. But, not everyone experiences this and inequities persist. In the context of persisting inequities and a formal and conceptual separation of paid work from domestic and family environments through the industrialisation process, social fragmentation has increased in the present.

The bottom right quadrant indicates that the present situation may lead in two directions. First, there may be an increase in the harmonisation between paid work and personal life maintaining personal freedom and attention to diversity (see top right quadrant). Or, second, a plunge into a crisis or set of crises could occur (bottom left and right quadrants). The UN has already discussed crises of care emerging in many societies which has critical social consequences, threatens traditional cultures and exacerbates issues of poverty and well-being in many societies (UN, 1999). This bottom right quadrant, which incorporates crises of care giving and receiving, could result in long-term implications not only for the environment (already increasingly noted) but also long-term economic stability or stagnation (also gaining more attention). If such crises occur (and it may be that we are already very close to experiencing them), there are two possible emergent pathways. One, with higher levels of social cohesion but achieved through coercion and a loss of personal freedom or attention to diversity (bottom left). In the other, the crises may act as stimuli for increased harmonisation of paid work with personal lives without loss of freedom or attention to diversity of people's varying needs and experiences.

The "upside potential" involves a move from the present situation, either directly or via the stimulus of a crisis, to a condition which combines a high level of individual freedom and consideration for diversity with enhanced work–personal life harmonisation. The notion of "harmonisation" in relation to paid work with the rest of life is a common human aspiration, but it represents a new evolutionary direction for human society. Industrial society has enhanced individualism and increased social fragmentation, but it may also be on the brink of providing the tools and organisational forms for individuals to act and interact primarily through flexible distributed networks. The power of information technology could preserve individual self-expression, autonomy and effectiveness of action while providing social relatedness and support through group connection and interaction. This emergent future scenario—*diverse, equitable harmonisation*—would represent a move beyond the "mass production/mass market" solutions of the industrial era, to a new pattern of "individual-in-group" solutions which could transform both work and personal life, offering both greater social harmonisation and individual fulfilment.

MOVING FORWARD: CRITICAL QUESTIONS

So, how could forces move towards this more optimal "upside potential"? Critical questions, building on our original critical points holding back change, now need to be asked if people and societies are to move forward in optimal ways. They include:

• How can we overcome the apparent impossibility of *thinking of alternatives to the ways market economies are implemented* despite what current or emerging forms appear to be doing to personal relationships, general well-being and human dignity within societies?

- How can we work through and overcome resistance towards *thinking about deep identity issues that arise from changing relationships between men and women* in different societies and redistribute these roles more equitably and satisfactorily for those involved?

- How can we overcome the reluctance or even apparent lack of awareness of the *need to address workplace structures, cultures and practices and ways in which work is actually done* that persist in penalising people who make changes in their own working practices?

- How can we *overcome a focus on quick fixes* and see these issues in wider and more radical ways? In the medium or long run, this may be less time consuming.

- How can we overcome reluctance to *appreciate and address the complexity of change processes*, recognising that they need to occur at a personal or individual level, but also at all other levels including the cultural and systemic?

MOVING FORWARD: PRAGMATIC STRATEGIES

Action is necessary at the international level because of the increasing global connectedness among countries and people. This is very difficult and many feel unable to work at this level. But, to follow the thinking of the influential literary critic and post-structuralist thinker, Edward Said (1935–2003), who spoke of the need to be idealistic without having illusions of the difficulties this produces, the scenario group participants expressed the need to try to encourage people who work globally and international organisations, such as the International Labour Organisation (ILO), World Trade Organisation (WTO), and the World Health Organisation (WHO), to think about and take on these issues.

But, while it is vital to think globally and widely about work–personal life harmonisation issues and to consider the critical questions highlighted above, it is also essential to harness pragmatic actions and strategies for change at local levels. It may be possible that actions at a number of levels could stop or mitigate the emerging crisis or set of crises or even turn them into something positive.

Action is also necessary within different societies and at all levels. It requires action from and collaboration between:

- *Governments* that need to consider how to respond to changes in families, work, workplaces and communities.

- *Workplaces* seeking to recruit, retain, motivate and utilise talented and diverse workers.

- *Trade unions* who want to make themselves relevant to the issues and discontents facing people in workplaces today.

- *Communities* hoping to revive local participation and civic spirit.

- *Families*, households and people in intimate relationships who value equity, companionship, friendship and connectedness.

- And *individuals* in the everyday organisation of their lives.

The international scenario meeting participants were eager to identify pragmatic actions to bring about change at each level. However, these must be considered within the complex situations and debates in diverse contexts and it is not possible to be prescriptive about the precise course of action for diverse stakeholders. Therefore, we briefly consider below some of the areas where pragmatic actions in some contexts could contribute to systemic sustainable change in the future and mention a few generic principles associated with these.

Government-level Actions

Legislation has a role at many levels: in supporting people with caring responsibilities; introducing or raising levels of minimum wages; and developing legislation in relation to working times, for example. There is also a need for governments—and wider societies—to develop and appropriately implement strategies in collaboration with people in their own countries as well as with other countries. This requires trust and mutual dialogue.

Legislation on Leave

- Statutory leave entitlements, such as parental leave, though not universal, are more generous or well established in some countries than others. However, there is a gap between policies and implementation in practice in most contexts and it is important that policy is supported and appropriately implemented at the workplace level. If such leave were available and acceptable not only for people with specific caring responsibilities but also for others regardless of family circumstances, this would require a radical rethinking of the way work is carried out. It could result in positive systemic change, involving widespread challenging of outdated norms and assumptions that operate at structural, cultural and practice levels. This kind of change, that recognises a variety of personal life needs or wishes, could bring greater equity for a variety of people. It could also mitigate potential backlash against mothers, parents or other carers who currently make use of special provisions.

Legislation on Working Time

- Maximum working hours vary considerably across countries. Many governments and organisations fear legislation on maximum working times may be detrimental to their economy. However, this does not take account of the possibility that if people worked differently they could be more effective in less time.

Legislation and Mechanisms to Support Carers

- Public policy support for carers also varies cross-nationally and this has a major impact on the harmonisation of paid work and personal life. Support for carers in diverse contexts within countries is essential. But, we also need to consider the impact of globalisation and international trade policies on carers around the world and particularly in developing countries where extended working hours and lack of care support can put the life of family members in danger (see, e.g., Heymann, Earle & Hanchate, 2004).

Introducing Minimum or Living Wages

- A realistic minimal living wage is a basic necessity for equitable and sustainable harmonisation of work and personal life. It is important to continue to address this challenge in each country as well as within international organisations, such as the ILO and the WTO.

- Introduction of a minimum wage is emerging in some contexts. This needs to be enhanced and developed so that people do not need to work around the clock simply to make ends meet. How to do this will vary in different countries. Difficulties will also emerge between countries, particularly given outsourcing and globalisation trends. This requires working through so as to enhance the benefits without producing negative costs, such as unemployment.

But, while we want to stress legislation is essential, it is mainly facilitative. It is necessary but not sufficient on its own and its aims often fail when it is not implemented appropriately at different levels of society. There is a need to think about implementation of initiatives, in terms of what is required to make legislation or government initiatives successful and how to get optimal impact.

Workplace-level Actions

One of the major problems of work–personal life harmonisation currently stems from workplace expectations and assumptions about what is a committed and competent employee. Outdated and gendered assumptions about "ideal workers"—as those who have no other responsibilities in life and can put the job first no matter what—remain. It is now important to move beyond the quick fix by tackling these persisting—but outdated—assumptions (see, e.g., Rapoport et al., 2002).

Tackling Persisting Myths or Outdated Assumptions about "Ideal" Employees

- Dialogue and collaboration is required in organisations about how to move forward from current working practices and persisting assumptions about "ideal" workers. Most employees do not have wives at home full time. But, many workplaces continue to operate as if they do. To be seen as a committed and effective worker, and to manage intensified workloads, long hours and "face time" are often expected. This penalises women, men and families who have no full-time carers at home. Such assumptions or myths are being exported to non-Western contexts with critical social consequences.

• Workplace policies have been developed in many contexts to support the family and care needs and wishes of employees. But, those taking such initiatives still tend to be marginalised. This results in widespread inequities for women, and prevents many men from taking advantage of these initiatives. Hence, existing gender roles are reinforced. Outdated assumptions now need to be tackled systemically and culturally by encouraging dialogue and collaboration between men and women about why they find it hard to reconcile paid work with other parts of their lives, and how paid work could be done differently to accommodate a variety of personal life needs or wishes, regardless of family circumstances. It is time to move beyond the quick fix and tackle much more embedded assumptions about how to work and how to harmonise this better with personal lives.

Recognising and Using the Dual or Multiple Agenda

• Enhancing workplace effectiveness and equity does not have to be a trade-off. Evidence shows that collaboration between people already working together in organisations to develop new working practices, values and norms—that account for and respect personal life needs and workplace effectiveness—can bring positive results for both. For example, in a small manufacturing company that had made big losses, a new CEO turned the company around by paying attention to people's expressed personal needs. He recognised that it was a "backs to the wall" situation and that people were his greatest asset. He worked with them to create innovative working practices which would not only satisfy their personal needs but also enhance workplace effectiveness.

• Tackling outdated assumptions about "ideal" workers frees people to develop much more innovative ways of working that take account of both business and personal needs. Such an approach can be called a dual or multiple agenda. The dual agenda was developed in the context of exploring new ways of working that enabled greater gender equity and workplace effectiveness (see Rapoport et al., 2002). The dual agenda approach uses the premise that personal life and workplace needs are not antithetical. They impact on each other and both need attention in order to maximise the other. This approach takes time to begin with, and involves tackling deep identity issues, assumptions and resistances, which require guidance, collaborative leadership and support. But, we have since developed this approach to a multiple agenda that looks at a range of equity issues at several levels, including not only the workplace but also the community, family, interpersonal and individual (see Lewis, Rapoport et al., 2003).

• Leaders can also facilitate change by showing examples of work–personal life harmonisation awareness and practice, and in recognising the importance of relational skills.

Sustainable Corporate Governance

• Companies including multinationals are sensitive to pressures from consumers and investors. Evidence in some countries suggests people are willing to pay a bit more for fair trade products, and companies with ethical investment policies attract growing numbers of customers.

• If companies had to report publicly on their performance regarding finance, environment and people, they would become aware of bad publicity. They do not like this, particularly when it affects their share price and could encourage or generate change.

Trade Union-level Actions

Trade unions are beginning to recognise that work–personal life harmonisation is a major issue for men and women and some are increasingly pushing for greater rights for time for other activities in life. Yet, many, particularly those which remain very male-dominated, have been slow to take up such an agenda. Addressing work–personal life harmonisation issues from a global and local perspective is key, and trade unions need to play a part.

Staying Relevant in a Modern World

• If unions, whose support and membership continues to dwindle in many countries, want to make themselves relevant to the needs of people and assert modern-day relevance, they will need to follow the example of those unions that place work–personal life issues at the top of their agendas (see *www.tuc.org.uk/changingtimes*).

Addressing National/International Tensions

• Unions have to confront dilemmas about the rights of workers in their countries and those of workers in other countries. A reassessment and step towards inter-country collaboration—evident in some unions—needs to occur as the labour market becomes more and more connected.

Community-level Actions

In many societies, current or emerging discontents about work–personal life harmonisation also feed into and are affected by concerns around a decline in community participation and sense of belonging. "Overwork" is a major reason cited for decline in community participation (see Putnam, 2000[4]), because many have less time to spend in their localities or to engage in communities that matter to them. Current patterns of work, often away from community contexts (e.g., with long commutes), or involving short-term, episodic labour in the new flexible capitalism (see Sennett, 1998) can also perpetuate this erosion.

---

[4] Although Bookman (2003) argues that in the USA people are finding time for community—but it's not the organised kind, instead it centres on schools, churches, etc.).

Tackling Community Decline

- Restoring a sense of belonging within fragmented communities is at the heart of several emerging initiatives across the Western world. One response is to require that people be freed up from some paid work for voluntary activities as part of corporate social responsibility programmes (see Bookman, 2004), and these can be useful. However, it is important that corporate social responsibility is not just used as another quick-fix mechanism for avoiding examining working practices and the assumptions on which they are based.

Recognising and Using a Dual or Multiple Agenda across Civil Society

- Actions at civil society levels also need to utilise a dual or multiple agenda approach, seeking solutions that meet the needs of individuals and families, of workplaces and of communities. Community supports and practices are often based on the assumptions that there is a family member (usually a mother or other female carer) at home. School structures, cultures and practices, for example, need to examine assumptions about families of children. It would be helpful for parents, teachers and children to work collaboratively on issues, such as school hours, holidays and the ways teaching gets done. A similar approach could be adopted across a range of public bodies and professions, including health and social care.

New Community Systems

- Skills exchanges are emerging in some communities in which the talents or resources of different community members are exchanged instead of paying for services and resources. These range from care provision to water plumbing, and need to be utilised and encouraged in a variety of community settings (see Letslink UK, 2003).

- It is important to recognise that communities vary in nature. Communities are not only formed on the basis of where people live, but also where people work, socialise or worship spiritually. For example, communities can be formed at churches, at mosques or at schools.

Family-level Actions

At the family level, gender and other inequities permeate. These need to be worked through with collaborative dialogue and mutual understanding. Such strategies require legislative and workplace support, but this does not address many of the difficulties people face in making such changes. Issues of identity and resistance or fear are widespread: men can be reluctant to give up power or status derived from the world of paid work, and women can fear giving up power in the home or the identity they derive from nurturing and caring roles. Tackling these issues is crucial.

Sharing and Valuing Care

- The sharing of care, connectedness, leisure, well-being and financial sustainability between women and men, or those with same sex partners, requires mutual and honest dialogue at the family level. It can be very difficult for men and women to take on behaviours "traditionally" regarded as belonging to the "other" gender in workplaces, communities or families. Action research in the US is currently pioneering a shared care programme that seeks to work with people at the family level to encourage men and women to collaborate in trying to resolve tensions arising amongst families by seeking new forms of care and family arrangements (Degroot & Fine, 2003; *www.thirdpath.org.uk*). This has had positive results and the general approach could be built upon in appropriate ways in other contexts.

- A complementary path, supported through government benefits or workplace allowances, could also ensure that care providers are financially rewarded and skills developed through caring activities become recognised and rewarded in the workplace.

Individual-level Actions

While work–personal life harmonisation discontents are largely systemic issues rooted in such factors as entrenched social power relations
including the gender imbalance, the nature of industrial economies,
and global competition, some responses are possible at the individual
level.

Rejection and Renewal

- If growing numbers of people reject or rebel against current forces by
  altering the ways in which they harmonise paid work with the rest of
  their lives—a trend that seems to be emerging—the system will eventually be forced to change.

- People can reject conditions that are no longer appropriate and cele-
  brate trade-offs between higher individual material standards of living
  and other ambitions of men, women and societies, whether spiritual,
  ecological, cultural or social.

- But, such action assumes people have the financial capacity to act in
  this way, and requires collective actions as set out at other levels of
  societies to ensure more people—regardless of their socio-economic
  position—can take such steps.

MOVING FORWARD: NEW ALLIANCES

Currently, many people feel lost, pedalling in a hopeless direction.
Some feel there is no alternative to carrying on along the same path:
that it has to be this way. But, alternatives are beginning to emerge from
environmental and sustainable development movements. We can learn
from successful social movements about how to enact optimal change,
and new alliances need to be formed. Essentially, emerging social
movements and trends are exploring whether there is a different way
to live. An emphasis on sustainability of prosperity, the environment

and people can forge new alliances. This may help to challenge
the primacy of unfettered economic growth and consumerism that
fails to pay attention to the well-being of people and societies more
generally.

References

Argyris, C. and Schon, D. (1991). Participatory action research and action science compared. In: W. Whyte (ed.), *Participatory Action Research*. London: Sage Publications.

Ayree, S., Luk, V. and Stone, R. (1998). Family responsive variables and retention: Relevant outcomes among employed parents. *Human Relations*, **51**(1), 73–87.

Bailyn, L. and Fletcher, J.K. (2003). *The Equity Imperative: Reaching Effectiveness through the Dual Agenda* (CGO Insight #18). Boston: Center for Gender & Organization.

Barnett, R. (1994). *The Limits of Competence*. Milton Keynes, UK: Open University Press.

Bevan, S., Dench, S., Tamkin, P. and Cummings, J. (1999). *Family-friendly Employment: The Business Case* (DfEE Research Report RR136). London: Department for Education and Employment.

Bookman, A. (2004). *Starting in Our Own Backyards: How Working Families Can Build Community and Survive the New Economy*. New York: Routledge.

Brandth, B. and Kvande, E. (2001). Flexible work and flexible fathers. *Work, Employment and Society*, **15**(2), 251–267.

Brandth, B. and Kvande, E. (2002). Reflexive fathers: Negotiating parental leave and working life. *Gender, Work and Organization*, **9**(2), 186–203.

Brannen, J., Lewis, S., Nilsen, A. and Smithson, J. (2002). *Young Europeans, Work and Family*. London: Routledge.

Bunting, M. (2004). Willing slaves. In: C. Cooper, S. Lewis, J. Smithson and J. Dyer (eds), *Flexible Futures: Flexible Working and Work–Life Integration*. London: Institute of Chartered Accountants in England and Wales.

Cohn, R. (1983). *Van Psychanalyse naar Themagecentreerde Interactie*. Amsterdam: H. Nelissen Baarne.

DeGroot, J. and Fine, J. (2003). Integrating work and life: Young women forge new solutions. In: *The American Woman 2003–2004: Daughters of a Revolution—Young Women Today*. New York: Palgrave Press. Available at *www.thirdpath.org*

Dex, S. and Schreibl, F. (2001). Flexible and family friendly working arrangements in UK-based SMEs: Business cases. *British Journal of Industrial Relations*, **39**(3), 411–431.

DTI (2001). *Work–Life Balance: The Business Case*. London: Department of Trade & Industry.

Eden, C. and Huxham, C. (1999). In. R. Clegg and C. Hardy (eds), *Studying Organisations*. London: Sage Publications.

Felstead, A., Jewson, N. and Walters, S. (2003). Managerial control of employees working at home. *British Journal of Industrial Relations*, **41**(2), 241–263.

Fletcher, J. and Rapoport, R. (1996). Work–family issues as a catalyst for organizational change In: S. Lewis and J. Lewis (eds), *The Work–Family Challenge* (pp. 142–158). London: Sage Publications.

Folger, R. and Kanovsky, M. (1989). Effects of procedural justice, distributive justice, and reactions to pay raise decisions. *Academy of Management Journal*, **32**, 115–130.

Gambles, R., Lewis, S. and Rapoport, R. (forthcoming). *Work–Personal Life Harmonisation*. Chichester, UK: John Wiley & Sons.

Haas, L. and Hwang, P. (1995). Company culture and men's usage of family leave and benefits in Sweden. *Family Relations*, **44**, 28–36.

Heymann, J., Earle, A. and Hanchate, A. (2004). Bringing a global perspective to community, work and family: An examination of extended work hours in families in four countries. *Community, Work and Family*, **7**(2), in press.

Hibbert, A. and Meager, N. (2003). Key indicators of women's position in Britain. *Labour Market Trends*, **11**(10), 503–511.

Hochschild, A. (1997). *The Time Bind: When Work Becomes Home and Home Becomes Work*. New York: Henry Holt.

Lee, M., MacDermid, S. and Buck, M. (2000). Organizational paradigms of reduced load work: Accommodations, elaboration and transformation. *Academy of Management Journal*, **43**(6), 1211–1236.

Letslink UK (2003). UK LETS and complementary Currencies Development Agency. Available at *www.letslinkuk.org*

Lewis, S. (1997). Family friendly organizational policies: A route to organizational change or playing about at the margins. *Gender, Work and Organisation*, **4**, 13–23.

Lewis, S. (2001). Restructuring workplace cultures: The ultimate work–family challenge? *Women in Management Review*, **16**, 21–29.

Lewis, S. (2002). Current trends in work–life research. In: R. Burke and D. Nelson (eds), *Advancing Women in Corporate Management*. Oxford, UK: Blackwell.

Lewis, S. (2003a). Flexible working arrangements. In: C. Cooper and I. Robertson (eds), *Annual Review of Industrial and Organisational Psychology* (pp. 1–28). Chichester, UK: John Wiley & Sons.

Lewis, S. (2003b). The integration of paid work and the rest of life: Is post industrial work the new leisure? *Leisure Studies*, **22**, 343–355.

Lewis, S. and Cooper, C. (1999). The work–family research agenda in changing contexts. *Journal of Occupational Health Psychology*, **4**(4), 382–393.

Lewis, S., Brannen, J. and Smithson, J. (1999). Young Europeans' orientations to families and work. *Annals of the American Academy of Political and Social Science*, **562**, 83–97.

Lewis, S., Cooper, C., Smithson, J. and Dyer, J. (2003). *Flexible Futures*. London: Institute of Chartered Accountants in England and Wales.

Lewis, S., Kagan, C. and Heaton, P. (2000). Family diversity for parents of disabled children: Beyond policy to practice. *Personnel Review*, **29**(3), 417–430.

Lewis, S., Rapoport, R. and Gambles, R. (2003). Reflections on the integration of paid work with the rest of life. *Journal of Managerial Psychology*, **18**(8), 824–841.

Nonaka, I. and Takeuchi, H. (1995). *The Knowledge Creating Company*. New York: Oxford University Press.

Parasuraman, S. and Greenhaus, J. (1997). *Integrating Work and Family: Challenges and Choices for a Changing World*. Westport, CT: Quorum.

Peper, B., Lewis, S. and Den Dulk, L. (2004). Reconciling work and parenthood in the new European workplace: The role of colleagues. Paper presented at *Conference on Work–Life Balance, University of Edinburgh*.

Poster, W.R. (2004). Organizational change, globalization, and work–family programs: Case studies from India and the United States. In: S.A.Y. Poelmans (ed.), *Work and Family: An International Research Perspective*. Mahwah, NJ: Erlbaum.

Prutchno, R., Litchfield, L. and Fried, M. (2000). *Measuring the Impact of Workplace Flexibility*. Boston: Boston College Center for Work and Family.

Putnam, R. (2000). *Bowling Alone: The Collapse and Revival of American Community*. New York: Touchstone.

Rapoport, R., Bailyn, L., Fletcher, J. and Pruitt, B. (2002). *Beyond Work–Family Balance: Advancing Gender Equity and Work Performance*. Chichester, UK: John Wiley & Sons.

Rapoport, R., Lewis, S., Bailyn, L. and Gambles, R. (2004). Globalization and the integration of work with personal life. In: S.A.Y. Poelmans (ed.), *Work and Family: An International Research Perspective*. Mahwah, NJ: Erlbaum.

Scandura, T. and Lankau, M. (1997). Relationship of gender, family responsibility and flexible work hours to organisational commitment and job satisfaction. *Journal of Organizational Behavior*, **18**, 377–391.

Senge, P. (1990). *The Fifth Discipline: The Art and Practice of the Learning Organization*. New York: Doubleday.

Senge, P., Kleiner, A., Roberts, C., Ross, R., Roth, G. and Smith, B. (1999). *The Dance of Change: The Challenge of Sustaining Momentum in Learning Organizations*. New York: Doubleday.

Sennett, R. (1998). *The Corrosion of Character*. New York: W.W. Norton.

Sullivan, C. and Lewis, S. (2001). Home-based telework, gender and the synchronisation of work and family: Perspectives of teleworkers and their co-residents. *Gender, Work and Organisation*, **8**(2), 123–145.

UN (1999) *The Invisible Heart—Care and the Global Economy* (United Nations Human Development Report). Oxford, UK: Oxford University Press.

Van den Bogaard, J., Callens, I. and van Iren, A. (2003). *On Linking the Quality of Work and Life*. The Hague: Netherlands Ministry of Social Affairs and Employment.

Webster, J. (2004). *Working and Living in the European Knowledge Society: The Policy Implications of Developments in Working Life and Their Effects on Social Relations* (Report for the project "Infowork: Social Cohesion, the Organisation of Work and Information and Communication Technologies: Drawing out the lessons of the TSER research programme and the Key Action on Socio-economic Research"). Brussels: EU.

Young, M.B. (1999). Work–family backlach: Begging the question, "What's fair?" *Annals of the American Academy of Political and Social Science*, **562**, 32–46.

Index